QUILT INSPIRATIONS
from AFRICA

Quilt Inspirations
from Africa

A Caravan of Ideas, Patterns,

Motifs, and Techniques

KAYE ENGLAND & MARY ELIZABETH JOHNSON

THE QUILT DIGEST PRESS
NTC/Contemporary Publishing Group

Library of Congress Cataloging-in-Publication Data

England, Kaye.
    Quilt inspirations from Africa : a caravan of ideas, patterns, motifs, and techniques /
Kaye England and Mary Elizabeth Johnson.
       p.   cm.
    ISBN 0-8442-4206-3
    1. Quilting—Africa—Patterns.   2. Patchwork—Africa—Patterns.   3. Quilts—Africa.
I. Johnson, Mary Elizabeth.   II. Title.

TT835.E53   2000
746.46'041—dc21   00-21297
                                                               CIP

Editorial direction by Anne Knudsen
Art direction by Kim Bartko
Project editing by Craig Bolt
Book design by Susan H. Hartman
Cover design by Monica Baziuk
Drawings by Mario Ferro
Manufacturing direction by Pat Martin

Published by The Quilt Digest Press
An imprint of NTC/Contemporary Publishing Group, Inc.
4255 West Touhy Avenue, Lincolnwood (Chicago), Illinois 60712-1975, U.S.A.
Printed in Hong Kong by Midas Printing, Inc.
International Standard Book Number: 0-8442-4206-3
 01 02 03 04 17 16 15 14 13 12 11 10 9 8 7 6 5 4 3 2 1

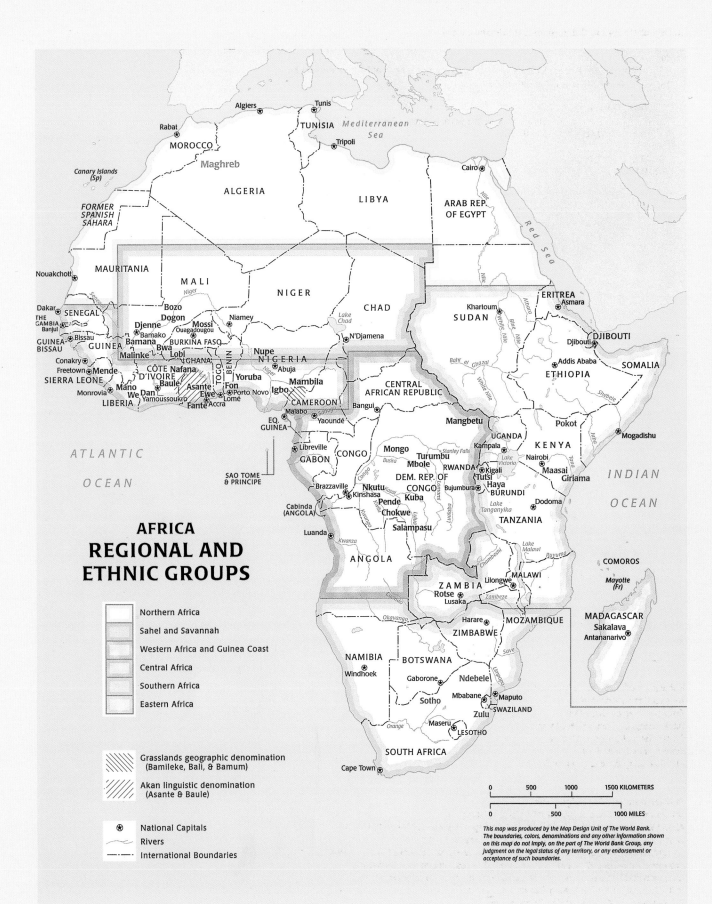

AFRICA
REGIONAL AND
ETHNIC GROUPS

Northern Africa

Sahel and Savannah

Western Africa and Guinea Coast

Central Africa

Southern Africa

Eastern Africa

Grasslands geographic denomination
(Bamileke, Bali, & Bamum)

Akan linguistic denomination
(Asante & Baule)

⊛ National Capitals

〜 Rivers

—·—·— International Boundaries

0   500   1000   1500 KILOMETERS

0   500   1000 MILES

This map was produced by the Map Design Unit of The World Bank.
The boundaries, colors, denominations and any other information shown
on this map do not imply, on the part of The World Bank Group, any
judgment on the legal status of any territory, or any endorsement or
acceptance of such boundaries.

IBRD 29012
APRIL 1998

◀ CRAZY FOR AFRICA
by Kaye England, 1999.
62" × 80" (158 cm × 203 cm).
Mysterious eyes look out at you—are they human or animal? Exotic beasts hide in forests of fabric. Dancers in masks and shields slip into view and out again. This quilt is so lively you can almost hear music playing. Of all the quilts in this book, it probably represents the patchwork that is Africa most completely, for Africa is a land of many parts, parts that do not always fit together smoothly. Yet, over the centuries, the many different ethnic groups lived alongside each other fairly well most of the time, for there was enough land, with little enough population, for everyone's needs.

Contents

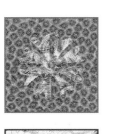

Part Two
A Caravan of Quilts 61

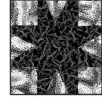

Acknowledgments

We benefited from the work of many others as we researched and produced this book. Our initial forays into the world of African art and design were taken through the stunning photographs and compelling text of many wonderful books, and we are grateful to those authors and photographers who searched out the mysteries of Africa. They often endured primitive traveling conditions and physical discomfort to give the rest of us an easy-chair glimpse of great wonders. Especially inspiring has been the work of Angela Fisher, Gary van Wyck, Margaret Courtney-Clarke, Laure Meyer, Suzanne Blier, Duncan Clark, John Picton, John Mack, and Roberta Horton. We have relied heavily on the Dover books of African design motifs. These references are listed in detail in the bibliography.

The same is true of the museum and gallery exhibitions we visited in preparation for this undertaking. Other brave and adventurous souls sought out the artifacts that pique the curiosity and invite scholarly exploration of cultures vastly different from our own. Two exhibitions in particular were helpful: the Birmingham Museum of Art's "Chokwe! Art and Initiation Among Chokwe and Related Peoples," and "Ndebele Images" at the Atlanta International Museum. Each show brought a closer focus to concepts we had read and studied, and it was thrilling to be in the presence of objects we had seen only in photographs.

As we cast our net for others interested in making quilts with an African theme, we made quite a catch. We are grateful to all those quilt artists who loaned pieces for photography and exhibition: Shelley Aff, Laurie Barnett, Alice Calhoun, Geneva Carroll, Jennifer Dwiel, Anita Gwin, Kathy Gwin, Terri Gunn, Anita Harden, Roberta Horton, Laurie Keller, Terrie Mangat, Lois McArthur, Peggy McKinney, Judy Pleiss, Teddy Pruett, Susan Raban, Cynthia Sochar, Sandy Heminger, Caryl Schultz, Martha Porch, and Anne Gallo.

Our friends Becky Hancock and Holice Turnbow contributed important sections to the book. Becky makes frequent trips to Africa to search out authentic beads and fabrics to sell in the American market. In the process, she has become quite an expert on many different African cultures, and she very generously shared her knowledge with us and loaned many of her artifacts (and stock) for photography. Holice, who lived in Africa, enthusiastically took to the suggestion of designing a line of African quilting motifs for this book and has also seen to the manufacturing of quilting stencils of the same designs for those of us who don't want to cut our own.

Many of the techniques featured on these pages are derived from the work of Mary Ellen Hopkins. Mary Ellen has been a leader in developing new and simpler ways to construct basic quilt blocks; her keen eye picks out basic building units that make each design much easier to construct than traditional methods. She developed the idea of "connectors," among other make-it-easy methods. Thank you, Mary Ellen, for your foresight and ingenuity!

When it came to meeting photography deadlines, Kaye was able to call on some especially talented friends who quilted their little hearts out when time was short: Alice Cunningham, Melissa Taylor, and Mary Jane Parvey. They made it possible for us to be on time for what sometimes seemed like impossible expectations. Several other pieces in the book were quilted with help from Veronica Schlosser, Cathy Franks, and Leona Berg.

Both of us are enormously happy to have our book published by The Quilt Digest Press. We consider it the crème de la crème of quilt book publishers, and it is our pleasure to be part of its program. The credit for the success of this book must go in great part to the hard work of Anne Knudsen and Craig Bolt, our editors, and to all the other fine people at The Quilt Digest Press. Thank you all.

This engraving, "Mtsea's Amazons," was taken from a photograph Henry M. Stanley made during his 1898 exploration of Uganda. In describing the Emperor's people, the Waganda, Stanley said they were tall and slender and that he had seen hundreds of them taller than 6′2″, including one who was 6′6″. They were of superior intelligence, he said, and possessed a "general love of cleanliness, neatness, and modesty," looking with distain on those who went about naked. Illustration copyright © Stock Montage.

Preface

We began our African journey because we are dreamers who have fallen in love with the images of Africa. We are not scholars of Africa, nor are we of African heritage. We have been seduced by viewing African art, both in major museum collections and in exhibitions devoted to African art that frequently travel this country. We have read Isak Dinesen's very idealized memoirs of managing a coffee plantation in Kenya, which led her to write *Out of Africa*, and we have watched the movie version over and over again. We have thrilled to the sounds of Ladysmith Black Mambazo, with and without Paul Simon. We have, since childhood, been fascinated by the animals of Africa and watched every possible television show about them. We have pored over big coffee-table art books on Africa's natural beauty, on African art, on African people.

Most important, we have admired the work of quilters who have traveled to various countries in Africa and been inspired in their own art. We have sought out imported African fabrics and embellishments and have experimented with them in our own pieces. Finally, when we could no longer resist the urge to write this book, we researched the subject as exhaustively as we could with the resources at our disposal. Everything we have learned has made us understand how little we really know—as many professional scholars have said, Africa is not something one can learn about in only one lifetime.

Nonetheless, having experienced the richness of African art and its cultures, we do feel that we have somewhat of a context in which to place the distressing, often brutal, governmental upheavals and tragic natural disasters that are so much a part of Africa today. We have agonized when the political news in Africa has been of trouble; we have grieved over the scenes of drought and suffering we have seen on television news programs. However, it is not our place or purpose to comment on the problems of Africa; we are qualified only

▲ OUT OF AFRICA

by Kaye England, 1994.

50″ × 42″ (120 cm × 100 cm).
What would a person who's seen the
movie more than 50 times name one of
her first African-themed quilts? "Out of
Africa," of course! A batik panel of an
outdoor African marketplace nestles in
nicely with appliquéd flora and fauna—
even water fauna are represented.

to share our response to the beauty that is Africa and how it has
affected our work. We agree with Diana Landau of Sierra Club
Books, who wrote in a preface to *Isak Dinesen's Africa: Images of the
Wild Continent from the Writer's Life and Words*: "If Isak Dinesen's
Africa exists today chiefly through her words and through images
captured on film, there exists also a real, changing, troubled, yet still
magical Africa to be cherished, safe-guarded, and reclaimed."

It is our desire to continue our African journey with you; we
hope to open the door just a bit on what has been a wonderfully
exciting experience for us. Perhaps you will join us through the quilts
you make and the journey you may one day take to this most
mysterious of all the continents.

Kaye England
Mary Elizabeth Johnson

Part One

AFRICA
ONE TREMENDOUS
ADVENTURE

A Swiss photographer in 1958 traveled from Tunis on the Mediterranean across the Sahara to the equator and then from the equator to the very southern tip of the continent, the Cape of Good Hope. The second leg alone was 11,200 miles, and, although the group was traveling in a fleet of Willys (now Jeep) station wagons, the entire journey took 10 months. Of course, he was photographing and was not traveling strictly to cover distance quickly.

Looking back now on the entire journey, I feel that its salient feature is the almost incredible diversity of impressions. We crossed primeval forests where giant orchids grow, passed dying velds (grasslands) and endless sand dunes. For weeks on end we met hardly a living creature, and then emerged into the teeming life of big modern cities. We watched innumerable animals, from the tiny desert mouse in a forlorn tin hut in the middle of the Sahara to the huge hippopotamus and rhinoceros in the vast game reserves. We visited primitive Negro villages and modern production plants; we stood on the shores of three seas and encountered people of the most diverse races and colors; black, brown, and white, Pygmies and giants, naked savages and cultured town-dwellers. It all adds up to one tremendous adventure.

—Emil Schulthess, *Africa*, Simon and Schuster, New York, 1959, p. vii.

CHAPTER 1

Beginning the Journey into Africa

◀ CIRCLES OF LIFE,

by Kaye England, 1999.

52″ × 70″ (133 cm × 178 cm). Africa, the mother continent, retains its aura of mystery and intrigue, even at the dawning of the twenty-first century. It was the first continent to be formed, the one from which North and South America and Eurasia split, and is the birthplace of mankind. This quilt speaks of the fertility, abundance, and richness of life forms found in Africa's bosom, as well as of secrets yet to be revealed. There were three sources of inspiration: for the leafy vine of the left lower corner (it is named maqoapi), a painted mural on a Lesotho home; for the great beaked face in the lowest circle, a carved motif on a comb from the Congo; and for the flying geese motifs in the right border, the Zulu symbol for a male. The neck rings of Ndebele women and the beaded "long tears" they wear when their sons go off to initiation school are interpreted in the figure at the left. The masks and small figures speak of the warrior classes of African societies.

The Art of a Thousand Nations

When you first go to the well of African design, you might think it too deep, because there is so much to draw from. Indeed, you will have before you the heritage and art of an entire continent and the oldest civilizations known to humanity. Some of the surviving cave art, enormously appealing because of its simplicity and graphic direct-ness, is from the Stone Age—the earliest prehistoric human culture.

There are estimated to be hundreds of ethnic groups and 1,000 or so languages. Each has its own aesthetic. As Kwame Anthony Appiah has written, "The traditions of each society are recognizably distinct. Africa's creative traditions are various and particular. The central cultural fact of African life, in my judgement, remains not the sameness of Africa's cultures, but their enormous diversity."[1]

To complicate things even further, African design encompasses many points of view. Because it cannot be categorized, it is impossible to make generalizations about "African art."

Africa, perhaps more than any other continent, resists the application of any kind of homogenizing label to its art. Within its boundaries are civilizations that were working gold and other metals, building fabulous palaces, trading with Asia, and producing textiles of color and texture when Europe was in the Dark Ages. Kingdoms have risen, ruled, and fallen; many anthropologists believe that what we actually do know of the people of Africa's past is only a fragment of the whole. After all, Europeans explored Africa's interior only as recently as the mid-nineteenth century, and archaeology and anthropology have really just begun to search for clues to the past. As time goes on and more discoveries are made, we will all gain in knowledge and understanding about the power and sophistication of the ancient peoples of the continent and their legacy of art.

The Geography of Africa

Perhaps it makes the most sense to look at the art of the continent in terms of its physical environment, because certainly the available natural materials determined the type of art that could be produced.

Africa is a land of extremes—arid and wet, flat and mountainous, hot and cold. Although the equator passes through the midpoint of the continent, it does not cut it exactly in half. The "bump" on the western side and the "horn" on the eastern side increase the landmass of the northern hemisphere considerably. The climatic and vegetation zones duplicate each other north and south of the equator. There is the steaming jungle of the equatorial rain belt, where the temperature difference between the hottest and the coldest day of the year is less than one degree, and it rains every day like clockwork. Plants and animals love it, and the pygmy, who lives there as he has since prehistoric times, has had to cope with few human intruders. Great rivers, like the Niger and the Congo, flow out of the rainforests into the Atlantic and Indian Oceans.

THE VIEW FROM THE ESCARPMENT, by Teddy Pruett, 1998. 60″ × 38″ (152 cm × 97 cm). A fertile plain, teeming with plant and animal life, is an idealized view of what the Dogon overlook from their hideaway homes built into the Bandiagara cliffs of Mali. As the quilter explains, "I did not originally plan to make a landscape. I cut 'bricks' from fabrics that said 'Africa' to me. I laid them out in a vertical arrangement, loosely from light to dark. The fabrics were pulled by using a great tropical print for inspiration, but the inspiration fabric was finally deleted entirely. The format eventually changed from vertical to horizontal, with a definite light source. I played with the animals, but they needed a strong focal point, so the baobab tree was designed and added. The small group of trees in the background were cut from a batik shirt, and dyed 'by cotton ball' to match the hand-dyed tree. There was still something missing. I needed more depth. At the very last moment I found an old upholstery sample with the large cheetah and decided it was time to stop. I wanted a strong border to balance the strength of the tree, and devised this free-cut sawtooth, and quilted it in a primitive design, and added the wonderful yarns and seashells."

The longest river in the world, the Nile, flows from Africa's Great Lakes region, 10 degrees of latitude south of the equator, across the continent to its delta on the Mediterranean in northern Egypt. The course of some of the rivers takes them over incredible plunges. For example, Victoria Falls, on the border between Tanzania and Zaire, drops several hundred feet with a thundering noise that can be heard many miles away.

Next to the rainforest on the north and south are the savannas, or grasslands, where rainfall is enough to support large herds of grazing animals. In these veldts the pastoral lifestyle developed; some groups eventually built villages, settled down, and traded to obtain the items they could not make themselves. Other groups migrated with the seasons to graze their cattle, goats, and sheep.

The desert comes next, with the Sahara in the north and the Kalahari in the south. The deserts are home to hearty souls, among them the Tuaregs and the Moors of the Sahara, and the Bushmen of the Kalahari. Nomadic groups of the Sahara, some of whom run their own trade caravans from the Mediterranean countries inland, also trade with groups who live along the edge of the savannas.

Beyond the deserts on both the north and the south coasts of the continent are mountain ranges. They front onto the Mediterranean Sea in the north and the Indian Ocean on the south. Along the Mediterranean coast range the Atlas Mountains, and at the southeastern edge of South Africa are the Drakensberg, or Dragon, Mountains.

Because early Europeans believed the vast Sahara was an impenetrable barrier between the Caucasian Arabic peoples of the Mediterranean and the mostly Negro peoples south of the desert (the sub-Saharan peoples), they imagined Africa as completely sub-Saharan. This image has been hard to dislodge. As recently as 1994–95, when the Royal Academy of Arts in London was preparing an exhibition about the art of Africa as a whole, a lively discussion arose as to whether or not the art of Morocco, Algeria, and Tunisia (collectively known as the "Magreb," after the Arabic name for northwest Africa) could be included. These countries were thought of as the "Mediterranean cultural zone," as though that set them irrevocably apart from the rest of the continent. Egypt came under similar scrutiny. Because the cultures of ancient Egypt were so similar to the "Mesopotamian culture zone" of the Biblical Fertile Crescent, Egypt must therefore belong to the Near East.[2] However, there is no doubt that each of these four countries, no matter how much thinking is applied, is indelibly part of the continent of Africa, and each adds its own enormous trove of art to the mix.

The truth is that the Sahara could be, and had regularly been, crossed and recrossed. Two things made it possible: camels and oases, those spots of green around occasional water holes in the unforgiving hills of sand. Camels became a means of transport in the desert about the sixth century, when the Byzantines took the area away from the Romans. Trading routes, run mostly by Saharan nomads, including the Tuareg and the Moors, were developed between the Magreb and the Sahel, with camels as the transport. (*Sahel* is Arabic for "shore" and was used to indicate the edge of the desert. One writer has suggested that this name indicates that the desert was regarded as an ocean of sand, to be traveled like an ocean of water.)

◀ SERENGETI GARDEN,
by Caryl Schuetz, 1999. 39″ × 39″
(100 cm × 100 cm).
Africa's abundant animal life is the theme
of the central medallion of this quilt, in
a scene created with the technique of
raw-edge appliqué and cutouts from an
imported fabric. A watering hole is
suggested with the wavy horizontal
lines of the central fabric. A spectacular
border that incorporates many African-
themed fabrics provides colorful
counterpoint to the black-and-white
"snapshot" of the center.

Art and Religion

Islam entered the continent through the gateway of north Africa.
Arabs came to trade as early as the seventh century and spread the
word as they traveled south, thereby obeying one of the most
important tenets of their faith—converting others. It has been
suggested that so many native cultures of Africa converted to Islam so
quickly because it was good for business—if you don't know much
about the fellow you're dealing with, it's comforting to know that you
worship the same God. A less cynical, and surely more important,
reason is that Islam allows for great diversity, so it was possible for
Africans to adopt Islam and keep many of their traditional beliefs.

It should not be assumed that Islamic influence was limited to
West Africa as brought in by the Arabic trading caravans that crossed
the Sahara. As early as the eighth century, Muslim traders sailed the
Indian Ocean to the eastern coast of Africa: Swahili culture developed
from the intermarriage of the Arabic traders with the native Negro
groups (the trading language that developed is called KaSwahili).

Christianity came to most of Africa much later. There have,
however, been Christians in north Africa and Egypt since shortly after
the death of Christ. Though Islam replaced Christianity in most
ancient cultures, Christianity has retained a remarkable stronghold in
Ethiopia since the seventh century. Ethiopian church services today
feature uniquely African dancing and drumming, and the church has
produced its own distinctive style of art and architecture.

The second wave of Christianity arrived on Africa's shores with
the Portuguese traders in the fifteenth century. Although there were
quite a number of converts, including the king of the Kongo, who
became known in Portugal as Alfonse I, the church was not able to
spare the staff to maintain its missions in Africa, and there is little
remaining of those early efforts. What does survive are some
astonishing life-size bronze figures of the Virgin and St. Anthony of
Lisbon that were cast by Kongolese artists. The real inroads of
Christianity into Africa came with colonization; only when European
governments controlled the various countries could Christian
churches establish and maintain missions to care for their converts.

As Christianity's traditional symbols were adopted by native
cultures, they took on uniquely African characteristics. Beautiful
illuminated manuscripts, with African animals and human figures,
produced in Ethiopia are just one example. The Christian cross
became a much-interpreted motif, especially for metalworking. One
African cross has four short arms of equal length, which represent the
four corners of the earth or, in other interpretations, the crossroads

between this world and the land of the dead. The African cross is found in many design applications, the most notable being the Ethiopian rock church shown on page 9. Many scholars believe that the familiarity of Africans with the cross as an icon for the spiritual world was a determining influence on their acceptance of Christianity. In addition to the African cross, there are African crucifixes made by the Kongo in the sixteenth century that, although they employ the Latin cross (tall upright and shorter crosspiece), display a Christ figure with distinctly African features, sometimes accompanied by spirit figures from the indigenous religion, perching on the crossarm or kneeling at His feet.

Perhaps the strongest appeal of these two world religions in Africa, according to Dr. Jocelyn Murray, is their emphasis on the power of God.

> *There is a great deal of fear in traditional beliefs—fear of spirits and ancestors whose power to do evil seems to be exercised arbitrarily. This calls for a continued watch over one's actions, so that no unintended offense is committed. The high god was very remote, beyond the reach of man, for good or evil. But in Christianity and Islam the creator-god is preached as powerful and concerned with men and women: "Allah the compassionate," "God is love." Both religions . . . do unite their followers in a . . . fellowship.[3]*

The religion of the African is one of practical application. There is reason to believe that the adoption of Christianity by some of the early rulers was their effort to obtain more power from a heavenly being—a practical approach for someone who already had a strong belief system in place. African religion is communal, not individual. Its primary values are harmony and unity with kin and clan, including the ancestors and other spirits, and with the earth. The African has a modest sense of himself in relation to the universe—he has a great respect for the forces of nature, knows his place in the natural order of things, and does not try to conquer the earth.

Islam and Christianity directly influenced many aspects of African art. Two examples of architecture demonstrate the incorporation of Islamic and Christian motifs with native design

One of the most amazing examples of vernacular architecture in the world is the stone church of St. George at Lalibela in the remote mountain province of Welo, north of Addis Ababa, Ethiopia. It is actually the largest monumental sculpture in Africa and dates from 1190–1225. The plan of the church is in the shape of a cross and was carved deep into rock. First, a square ditch was dug into the rock, then the church was carved out. The roof of the church, at roughly 35 feet, is almost exactly level with the surrounding ground. One enters the church by walking down a ramp. There are 12 churches like this one in the area, and services are still held in them. Courtesy of Werner Forman Archives/Art Resource, New York.

sensibilities and materials: the Friday Mosque in Mali and the Ethiopian rock churches. Islamic design influences are evident in the mosque in West Africa, as Christian themes are unmistakable in the Ethiopian churches.

Centuries of Isolation, Followed by One of Colonization

Until the mid-nineteenth century, the continent lay mainly undisturbed and unexplored by Europeans. The exceptions were the exotic and mysterious cities along the Mediterranean coast—Algiers, Tunis, Tripoli. Other coastal cities along the west African coast, such as Dakar in Senegal and Accra in Ghana, were brisk trading ports and departure points for the slave trade. Although many powerful African kings sold their neighbors and, sometimes, their own people, into slavery, the interior of Africa remained for the most part remote to the Europeans, although Europeans eventually bought more slaves than did the Arabs and others who had held slaves for centuries.

Europeans were always interested in locating the source of the Nile, and explorers from England, France, Belgium, Germany, and

Portugal journeyed forth to find it. The story of Livingstone and Stanley is of particular interest to Americans, since Stanley was an American newspaper reporter with the *New York Herald*—his editor sent him to Africa to find Livingstone. However, in the overall history of the continent, the European exploration of Africa was very recent.

Mid-nineteenth century explorations (fascinating to read about) led the way for European nations to further their interests on the continent, primarily extracting the wealth of raw materials from the interior and spreading Christianity through missions. Europeans divided Africa according to their economic interests. They established colonies and marked countries with borders that almost always had nothing to do with the homelands of the indigenous peoples. These newly formed countries were named for the nations that colonized

Native materials and building techniques were used to construct a mosque in Mopti, Mali, where the call to prayer goes out from the minaret. The men of Islam gather to pray together on Fridays, the holy day, although individual prayer is an expected part of daily life. In discussing the particular African nature of this mosque, one writer discoursed on the play of light across the mud walls and how it is enhanced by the shadows cast from the protruding ends of the timbers. Friday Mosque; Mopti, Mali. Photograph copyright © Georg Gerster/Photo Researchers.

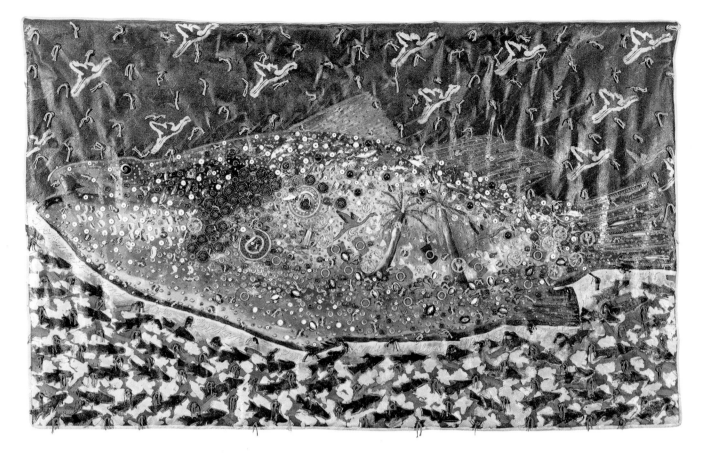

Lake Turk and Perch

by Terrie Mangat, 1990. 42″ × 42″
(107 cm × 107 cm).

Not all of Africa lacks for water; there are numerous lakes in addition to the powerful rivers that define much of its geography. This quilt was inspired by a fishing trip to Lake Turkana in northern Kenya; a fish-shaped island divides a horizon where flamingos fly and fish swim in the same direction. The piece is made of painted linen canvas and cotton print fabrics, embellished with beads and other objects, including a filleting knife, and is tied rather than quilted.

them—French Guinea, British Cameroon, Belgian Congo. The Sahel and Sahara became French; central Africa went mostly to the Belgians; eastern and southern portions became the provinces of the British; and the west was divided between the British and the French.

However, during the mid-twentieth century, many of these countries gained independence, sometimes after bloody revolts against colonial rule, sometimes after the ruling country abandoned its colonies. Establishment of self-rule has not always been easy; age-old rivalries among neighboring families or clans flared up. Often military dictators seized power and held it for many years, with grave consequences to the people of the country. Modern Africa is a continent in flux, politically, economically, and ecologically. However, there is much promise, based primarily on the concept of *ubuntu*, an intricate principle governing the way an individual relates to his community.[4]

According to *ubuntu*, the interests of the community come before the interests of the individual and the individual has responsibilities and duties to the community. It is an African way of thinking; it is the root of Africa's strong families and social customs, and it is a base of hope for the future of this great continent, which has already given the world so much beauty.

CHAPTER 2

African Design Inspirations

MASKERADE
by Kaye England, 1994. 42″ × 42″
(107 cm × 107 cm).
Exotic masks and the spirits they
represent provided the inspiration for
this quilt, which is rich with batik-type
fabrics, printed panels, and metallic
thread.

An Astonishing Creative Heritage

For anyone interested in looking at or creating beautiful things, Africa is an endless revelation. This continent of many ethnic groups, languages, religions, family traditions, cultures, and environments has, for thousands of years, produced items of incredible variety, sophistication, and beauty. Indeed, the African's sense of design has permeated all aspects of life. During the centuries before industrialization, when everything the African family used was made by hand of natural materials at great expense of labor and time, exquisite and intricate designs were incised into pottery, woven into mats and fabrics, carved into wood and ivory, and cast in metal.

Mali Dogon dancers. Photograph
copyright © Georg Gerster/Photo
Researchers.

13

A quilter will find endless inspiration and perhaps a fresh perspective by looking to Africa. The richness of design sources is awesome—piecing plans can be suggested by the design on a raffia basket; color schemes present themselves in the magnificent panoramas of mountains, sky, and grassy savanna; even learning a bit about how some of earth's oldest peoples viewed the world around them can stimulate a quilter's imagination in exciting ways.

African art and design encompass so many disciplines and traditions that we cannot possibly discuss them all. However, we believe that any work of art, including those that we as quilters make ourselves, is better understood when it is placed in a context. To understand those sources that have inspired the works in this book and to inspire you to begin your own search for African design inspirations, we present a brief overview of some of those aspects to which we, first as women, and second as fabric artists, can relate.

by Anita Harden, 1998. 50" × 52"
(127 cm × 132 cm).

The verticality of some ritual headdresses
is duplicated in the vertical strips of this
quilt. The quilt abounds in other African
motifs: the black and gold mud cloth
print at left, the stools in the black
background fabric at lower right, and, of
course, the scenic blocks containing
animals and a woman headed toward her
home, carrying a filled basket on her
head and her baby on her back.

Says the artist, "I identify with the
African women who carry their children
with them as they go about their daily
activities. That block is a tribute to them
and a reminder to me of a very precious
time in my son's and my life. Other
blocks were inspired by slides and
postcards of villages and landscapes. The
strong colors and geometric designs have
always appealed to me. I like
improvisation and free form a lot, but I
feel some order with the organization of
geometric designs. Call it my African
roots. I was fortunate to find so many
fabrics that appealed to those senses, but I
did have to modify some by slicing the
designs and creating the looks I wanted."

Religious and Social Influences on African Design

To begin, we must understand that the making of a piece of art has
historically been, in African terms, the solving of a problem or the
filling of a need. The motifs and objects that the Western eye
perceives as African "art" are usually made for a specific use that has
to do with a ceremony of some type—religious, political, or societal.
Many of the carved wooden figures and the elaborate masks we think
of as emblematic of African art were actually made for use in
religious ceremonies, as totems to bring good luck or blessings from
the spirits, or as charms to ward off evil forces. Much of the art has a
mystical or magical aspect, the true meaning of which is usually a
closely guarded secret, not known even to all members of the group.
Rites of passage, such as birth, circumcision, coming of age,
marriage, and death are occasions marked by much ceremony and
symbolism and with great variation among the ethnic groups.

Christianity and Islam and their motifs have, for many Africans,
been integrated into the native religions Africa has always known. As
they did with African art, scholars have looked for unifying elements
in the native African religions. The closest they have come to finding
any is with the concepts of ancestor worship and animism.

One scholar has suggested that a better name would be "living
force" for the link between the material and spiritual worlds that
animism addresses. Animism is the belief that everything in the
material world is inhabited by a spirit, and that these spirits are
personal. Consequently, each spirit must be treated differently
according to its particular characteristics or, if you will, its personality.

Ancestor worship is more rightly called reverence for the dead;
those relatives or clan members who have died are believed to be still
at hand and are remembered by name for two or three generations.
Their bones may be kept in a household altar, and gifts may
periodically be made to them. Because ancestors are seen as a link
between God in heaven and humans on earth, news of the clan is
reported to them. When misfortunes occur, a priest or witch doctor
may be consulted to ascertain whether or not the ancestor feels
ignored. Reverence for the dead was the impetus for building the
pyramids and performing the elaborate funerary rites for high-born
Egyptians. When they died, pharaohs and other notables joined the
ranks of those who interceded between beings still on earth and the
Ultimate Ruler, the God on High.

Spirits other than ancestors are worshiped. An ethnic group
of Mali, the Bambara, pays homage to the spirit who taught them

The Yoruba of Nigeria believe that the ancestral spirit known as Egungun has the power to determine the quality of their lives. Many of the masks and costumes synonymous with African art were made for the pageants and festivals devoted to ancestor spirits. These drummers' exotic masks and costumes and the spirits they represent provide the inspiration for "Maskerade" (page 12). Photograph copyright © Photo Researchers.

agriculture. This spirit is represented by an antelope whose name is *Chi Wara*. Other gods are in charge of rain and fertility during harvest season, and they are also represented by their own special symbol. Each culture has its own set of spirits and gods, but there is, interestingly, a similarity in the pantheon of deities among the ethnic groups.

Of great importance to Africans is their relationship to wild animals, for they believe that every animal has a spirit. Again, the animals held in esteem vary from group to group. The Senufo, for example, revere the five animals they believe to have been the first ones created: the chameleon, python, turtle, crocodile, and ground hornbill (a bird with a huge beak). The chameleon is an object of fear, because it changes color and has eyes that swivel in all directions; many charms are made in its image. The python is a fearsome snake believed to be a medium between man and the spirits; it is an ancestor of the Dogon race and is always featured in soothsayer's jewelry.[1]

The chameleon is also important to the Yoruba, because it also figures in their story of creation. They believe that God descended on a chain from heaven to the world, which was nothing but water and mist, poured out a gourdful of earth, and set a hen upon it. Everywhere the hen scratched, dry land was formed. A chameleon walked across the newly formed earth to test for firmness.

The interlocking worlds of African religions, parables, fables, and magic are too broad and rich for even a brief overview. Be assured,

CONTACTING THE SPIRIT WORLD

A witch doctor is a religious advisor whose function is to seek out the source of misfortune or evil and advise how it may be eliminated. He or she often is a healer who is conversant in the ways of natural medicine and herbs. In many belief systems, there are several ranks of spirits between the one creator of the universe and humans. For example, departed ancestors occupy the lowest rank in the spiritual world and may take the form of bush gods or other lowly positions. The function of the priest or witch doctor is to act as an intermediary between such spirits and humans. He or she uses many different rituals to communicate with and pacify the spirits, depending on the group to which the witch doctor belongs.

This recently made medicine bag was crafted in Nigeria by the Yoruba and has been used by one of their diviners. Each color and motif has a special meaning. Courtesy of St. Theresa Textile Trove, Cincinnati.

Witch doctors are held in high esteem in African society. The accessories that make up their costumes are designed for specific uses. This witch doctor is of the Luo people, of western Kenya. Photograph copyright © Carol Beckwith/Angela Fisher/Robert Estall Photo Library.

though, that you will spend many hours totally absorbed if you begin reading on these subjects. You will find that there are remarkable similarities in the tales we've always heard and the ones that Africans grow up with.

A Visual Feast—The Arts of the Ndebele

The Ndebele are a broad range of ethnic groups dispersed across Zimbabwe and the Transvaal province of South Africa, on the Indian Ocean side of the continent. This African word sounds like "in-de-belly," and the more the word is said, the more soothingly it lies on the tongue. Like so many of their African neighbors, the Ndeble have made artistic expression a part of their everyday lives, in their homes, their dress, and their personal adornment. The rich use of geometric forms is particularly striking in Ndbele designs. This, in itself, has instant appeal as a quilt inspiration.

The Ndebele live primarily on the savanna, in rectangular houses built of wooden poles covered with a mixture of mud and cow dung, the African stucco used by many other ethnic groups. Since the 1930s, the Ndebele women have painted the walls, both inside and out, of their homes and their fences. Their designs are strongly graphic, created of bold horizontal, vertical, and diagonal lines and marvelous deep, pure colors, such as gold, red, royal blue, forest green, and turquoise. Black and white are generously applied as accent colors. The Ndebele women mix traditional motifs, such as the sun and trees, with western symbols like the letters of the alphabet. They are ardent mimics—late twentieth-century shapes, such as razor blades, light bulbs, and telephone poles have found their way into Ndebele murals. Perhaps one of the most interesting twentieth-century icons they have adapted is the airplane, or more specifically, the jet, which they call the "ufly machine." They are also fond of the automobile because of the linear quality of the license plate and its numbers.

Many Ndebele women have turned their artistic talents to dollmaking for the tourist markets of South Africa. The doll, is not, however, a new idea; it has always played an important part of fertility rituals, not only with the Ndebele but with other groups as well. Doll from the collection of Kaye England.

Mothers teach their daughters how to paint during the three-month seclusion that accompanies puberty. Favorite family motifs are handed down from mother to daughter, and those motifs often find their way into the other cherished occupation of Ndebele women, beadwork. Many of the women who keep the old ways say that the real reason for painting the houses was to keep evil spirits at bay, not to decorate

▶ Stick Your Neck Out

by Lois McArthur. 41½″ × 53½″
(104 cm × 136 cm)

One of the most enduring images of
Africa is that of the Ndebele woman
with her graceful, elongated neck
encased in brass rings, and further
surrounded with thick straw rings that
have been completely encrusted in beads.
Her hair is very short, or her head is
shaved; one or more lovely beaded
headbands adorn the pate. This quilt
incorporates that image with other
familiar sights of Africa, and has a
happy, sunny quality because of all the
yellow fabrics.

the dwelling. Whatever the reason, the effect is dazzling—a true
visual feast.

Another passion of Ndebele women is beadwork, one they have
in common with the Yoruba, the Zulu, the Tutsi, and many peoples
of Africa. Beadwork was a tradition among the Ndebele for some 50
years before they began painting murals. Many favorite motifs were
transferred from one art form to the other; both use compact,
powerful shapes with symbolic connotations. Today many Ndebele
women apply these motifs to objects they make for the curio trade,
most notably dolls, animal figures, staffs, and household items.

They also continue to make the beaded garments that mark the
progression of a girl from childhood to womanhood; the oldest pieces
show beads that are small and predominately white. These old
garments were made of goatskin and the beads were sewn on with

sinew, but modern materials, even plastic sheeting and nylon thread, are used today. The colors of the beads do not seem to have any symbolic meaning, but each group of Ndebele has its favorite color scheme. However, white is nearly always dominant and is often the background for geometric motifs worked in color.

Perhaps the loveliest application of white beadwork is the headdress an Ndebele bride may wear, called a *siyaya*. It is a veil made of strands of white beads that completely encircles the head; although it is shorter in the front than in the back, it hides the face. The top is open, so that the crown of the head is visible.

▶ AFRICAN BLANKET

by Roberta Horton, 1995. 47″ × 72″ (120 cm × 183 cm). Machine pieced, appliquéd, and quilted, with additional sashiko quilting and hand-applied seed beads and glass ring beads. While visiting Ndebele women in South Africa, quilter Roberta Horton noticed that they wore a woolen blanket as part of their traditional clothing. When Roberta decided to design "African Blanket," she selected Nigerian tie-dyed indigoes and other African fabrics. "I love the crudeness of the tie-dye, which inspired me to quilt that area with large freehand stitches in sashiko thread," she comments. Photograph by Sharon Risedorph.

An Ndebele woman in South Africa wears a blanket that indicates she is married. She also wears the traditional neck and leg rings of brass, over which are rings of straw covered in beadwork. As she sits in a shady spot in the courtyard of the house she painted, her hands are busy with more beadwork. Photograph by Roberta Horton.

Young Ndebele initiates into manhood wear crossbands of white beads across their chests, along with white beaded headbands and legbands. The mother of each initiate signifies her status with a long panel of beadwork on either side of her face, which is attached to her headband or head covering; the Ndebele word for these accessories means "long tears," and suggests the anxiety the mother feels as her son leaves childhood and enters maturity.

African Beadwork

In ancient times, the Yoruba believed, as did other peoples, that buried beads would grow in the ground like plants. Another superstition, held by the Ashanti, is that some of the very old, rare, and treasured beads, made of powdered glass, could protect their owners in times of danger by barking like a dog; these same beads could also reproduce themselves. Of course, the truth of these beliefs could not be determined by the common folk, as only kings and chiefs could own these powerful beads, and the chiefs were permitted only one, which they would display prominently on cords around their arms.

Ancient beads of unknown origin, called "aggrey" have been found in the graves of chiefs and kings in West Africa, but they are rare; there is also evidence that Arabs traded beads of various materials across the Sahara as early as the ninth century. Glass beads

This young woman is a member of a nomadic Fulani group; she is stringing blue beads onto a wire to add to the marvelous decoration with which she is already adorned. Many nomadic groups beautify themselves, since they have no permanent homes on which to focus their creativity. Personal attractiveness is particularly important at the annual festival, when all the wandering groups gather, because young people find husbands and wives there. Many gold earrings and abundant cowrie shells and beads signal to prospective suitors that she is a woman of means. Angela Fisher/Robert Estall photographs, Suffolk England.

from Europe were introduced when the Portuguese established trade with Africa in the fifteenth century. Each African culture had its favorite bead; however, all loved the artistic Venetian beads that featured flowers, stripes, or mosaic designs, and everyone treasured gold beads, no matter what the style. By the twentieth century, "pound beads," the tiny ones that were traded by weight, had become especially popular. They were often unstrung and used with beads of many colors to make decorative objects.

Beads are important to young men in the Dinka and Maasai cultures. The Dinka wear a most unusual beaded corset: its colors change with the stages of their lives.[2] The Maasai wear colored beads as crossbands during initiation ceremonies. Beadwork among the Maasai is used to send messages, and often the sweethearts of the young men going through manhood rites send them off with beaded love tokens that only the two individuals themselves can decipher.

Royalty were, and still are, clad in fabulous beadwork in many parts of Africa, most notably in Nigeria and Benin, where 11 million Yoruba live today under the same traditions of kingship they have observed for centuries. Some of the most interesting objects to be found on the continent are the Yoruba kings' conical crowns of Nigeria. The shape calls attention to the head, which is the center of character, beauty, destiny, and spiritual power in the Yoruba belief system. The crowns are completely covered in beads and finished with sculptural birds, animals, and sometimes the faces of departed kings. A veil of beads finishes the crown and not only hides the king's identity but also saves the commoner from the perils of looking directly into the face of one so powerful. Additional royal accessories are wrought in beads: boots, leggings, staffs or scepters, and orbs, even thrones and cushions. Historically, a guild of specialized artists was kept under royal and priestly retainer to make such beadwork.

In the Cameroon grasslands, where the Bamileke, Bamum, and other families live, royal thrones carved from a single piece of wood more than five feet (1.5 m) high are completely covered with beads and cowrie shells. The word for the royal seat is *mandu yenu,* which means "a richness of beads." When these thrones were made, beads were very expensive and cowries were still being used like coins.

Vessels for serving palm wine are also an important accessory in the royal courts of Cameroon. These vessels often contain certain bones of royal ancestors, and drinking from such a container reinforces the notion that the king is endowed with a sixth sense, the ability to see beyond the natural world into the spirit world. Special craftsmen in the court cover long-necked gourds, or calabashes, with expensive beads and they fashion elaborate stoppers, also in beads, shaped like animals that symbolize royal authority, such as the leopard or elephant.

This beaded palm wine container, made before 1914, was used in the royal court of the Bamileke of Cameroon. The stopper represents a double leopard, a symbol of sovereignty. It is made of a gourd covered with beads and is nearly two feet tall. Photograph copyright © The Field Museum, Chicago, Ill. Neg. #109104C. Photograph by Fleur Hales Testa.

AN AFRICAN FASCINATION

by Becky Hancock

Beads and charms have been used for thousands of years in Africa for protection, spiritual empowerment, enlightenment, and adornment. In many cultures, beads and charms are an essential part of everyday life. Talismans are used to ward off evil spirits and for medicinal purposes, such as increasing fertility, virility, or lactation, or to keep blood flowing from wounds to cleanse them.

1 *Brass Pendants and Fetishes:* Assorted pendants and charms made in the Ivory Coast use the lost-wax method of casting metal. These are used for protection and also as standard weights for weighing gold. The mud fish is a symbol of nourishment and protection; the crocodile and turtle represent Mother Earth or the Queen Mother; the dog stands for cunning and shrewdness. A catfish represents danger, but a snake stands for good luck and prosperity.

2 *African Passport:* Wooden masks carved with particular tribal features are carried as a means of identification by tribesmen when traveling—like a passport.

3 *Evil Eye Piercer:* Made of horn, from Kenya, this is what I call the BMEEP: Big Mother Evil Eye Piercer! It is guaranteed to divert and attack any major evil forces coming at you.

4 *Hands:* The hands made of bone are from a small cottage industry in Kenya. I go there now, since the little elderly man from whom I used to buy wonderful bone beads and embellishments went blind and could no longer carry on his business. Hands are used primarily as protection from the evil eye, to stop it and put it out! They also represent vision and insight. Intricately decorated hands are often called the "Hand of Fatima," after the favorite daughter of Mohammed.

5 *Fertility Seed Necklace:* This necklace is worn before pregnancy to ensure conception, then during and after pregnancy to ensure a healthy baby. The white beads stimulate lactation in the new mother.

6 *The Foot of Change:* Portuguese slavers were responsible for establishing a huge population in Brazil of many African ethnic groups. Some of the more progressive Brazilian plantation owners established a step-by-step procedure by which slaves could win their freedom; a special symbol was awarded for each step. To celebrate their release from slavery and their step into a new life of freedom, many individuals carved this charm from wood and decorated it with silver or tin. They wore it along with the other symbols that proclaimed their emancipation.

7 *Fulani Wedding Beads:* These beads were made in the fifteenth century in the Czech Republic and traded to Africa. They are used primarily by the Fulani tribe; it is customary for a Fulani groom to present a strand of these beads to his bride on their wedding day. She will use them to embellish her clothing and headdresses. Some of the beads were made to resemble animal claws, which are thought to impart the strength of the animal to the wearer. These beads are also admired by Berber women.

8 *Doum Nut:* This is a palm tree nut from the coastal region of West Africa, sometimes called vegetable ivory. It is used as a carving material and is often made into beads, which can be used for adornment or as a spinning whorl by weavers.

9 *Amber Beads:* Amber is highly prized among Africans. It is used for healing, stimulation, energizing, increasing vision into spiritual matters, and for protection.

Genuine amber can acquire a static electrical charge, floats in salt water, chips easily, warms your hand, and gives off a piney scent when rubbed. Besides all that, amber is a sign of status and wealth when worn. It is also very expensive, currently selling for $8 (U.S.) per gram.

10 *Assorted Bone Fetishes and Pendants:* The animal shapes, or fetishes, are used to invoke protection, prosperity, and good luck. They take the shapes of fish, crocodiles, lions, dogs, frogs, turtles, snakes, elephants, and birds. The pendants are used for protection and adornment: they are shaped as crescent moons, fans, counting tablets, shields, gourds, teeth, feathers, thread bobbins, and pottery, among other things. Color is applied as desired to the different shapes.

11 *Trade Beads:* Assorted glass beads made in Venice in the nineteenth century that were traded to Africans for palm oil, diamonds, and gold.

12 *Masks:* These mask charms are made from brass, wood, and bone in the Ivory Coast, Mali, Zaire, and Kenya. Masks are very important in African ceremonial dances. They represent spirits and deities and protect the dancers from roaming spirits. Often masks are "smoked" to drive out any residential spirit that might be hanging around. Masks are sometimes made in the image of a dead relative in the hope that the wearer will take on the strengths and personality traits of the deceased (see the wooden mask with the long beard). The Baoule warriors of the Ivory Coast often make masks of conquered enemies and wear them as charms or put them on the handles of their swords.

13 *Small Striped Venetian beads:* Made in Venice in the 1800s, these beads are partic-

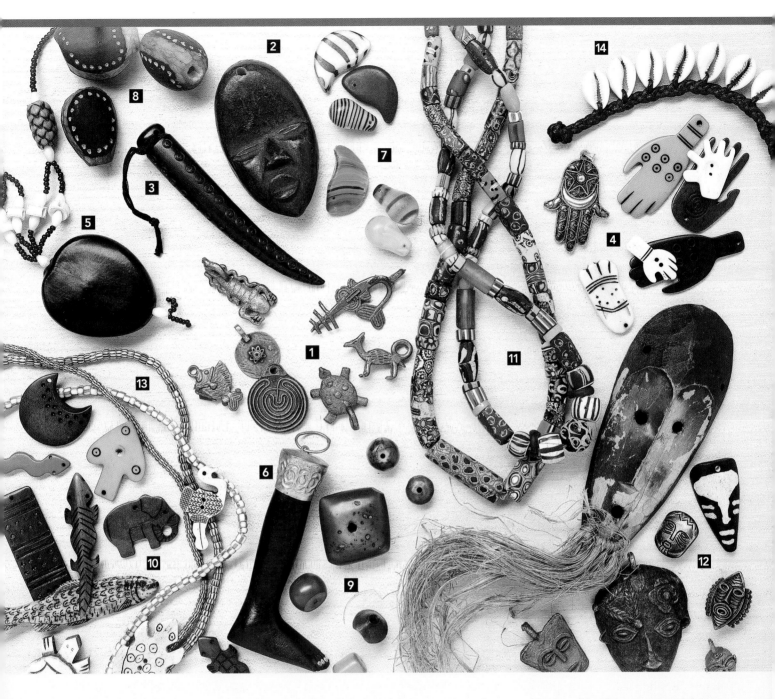

ular favorites of the Maasai, who use them in jewelry and sew them onto clothing.

14 *Cowrie Shells:* These are found on both the eastern and western coasts of Africa and are used extensively for embellishment. Because they were once used as a medium of exchange, they are sometimes called money shells. Although they are now used only for adornment,

they are thought to bring prosperity and good luck.

Diviners use cowrie shells to read the past, present, or future. A fortune teller in Africa used cowrie shells to do a reading. He gave me a formula for luck and prosperity, which seems to work for everyone who tries it. He said to take 17 cowrie shells (an uneven number brings luck and protection)

and let them "sleep" in water overnight; in the morning rinse your hair with the water. Then make a small gift of charity to someone, a friend or a stranger, and wear silver jewelry to attract good fortune and divert the evil eye. A friend had lost her car and her job; within a month of trying this formula, she had both! I have heard many other success stories since.

A Look at Today and Tomorrow

A fast-moving world presents only more change and more challenge to the traditional ways of African culture, which are rapidly falling before "progress." The traditional ways are often ridiculed by the younger generations; new, synthetic materials are coming into use as natural materials are gobbled up by international corporations or as the cities advance into rural areas.

All change is not to the detriment of the arts and crafts, though. Ndebele women developed their beadwork to assert their cultural identity when they were forced to migrate from their traditional homelands and resettle in the late nineteenth century. They later began painting murals on their houses. There are promising and exciting young artists working in both new and old ways to create stimulating work that reflects the contemporary environment.

MEMORIES OF KENYA

by Martha Porch, 1999. 60″ × 60″
(152 cm × 152 cm).

According to the quiltmaker, the most fantastic vacation she and her husband ever took was a safari to Kenya. In addition to visiting game reserves such as the Amboseli National Park, where they were delighted by a large elephant herd with Mount Kilimanjaro in the background, they were treated to tea in the afternoon and a roaring campfire at night. She recorded her memories of the trip in this quilt made with crazy patches and African-themed fabrics. The necklace of seeds and quills in the upper left corner was purchased in a Maasai encampment from a woman who made craft items to raise money for her children's education.

Traditional weavers, for example, are making exquisite use of new synthetic yarns, such as lurex, in contemporary fabrics. As we shall see in the next chapter, the ease of production of roller-printed fabrics now makes it possible for an African woman to step into a manufacturer's office and order a length that sends a specific message about her opinion on a particular subject.

The export trade teems with handmade reproductions of traditional forms. There is a brisk business in wooden masks and other items made specifically for export. Such items are not, of course, considered art, but are reproductions intended for the tourist or casual market. It is not unusual to find imported African crafts in cities all across the United States, many of them made expressly for export. Zulu beadwork such as necklaces and "love letters" worked on a safety pin keep company with dolls whose original purpose was to bring fertility to a bride. Masks, stools, headrests, orbs, and weaponry are reproduced and exported to America in great quantities. Fabrics from Africa are easily found; printed reproductions of kente cloth are sold alongside lengths of authentic mud cloth. Because these artifacts and materials are readily available, the quilter can more easily immerse herself in the culture of Africa.

Many traditions are kept, but with a modern touch. It is not unusual to spot a photograph of a king in a kente cloth toga with a Rolex wristwatch. News stories remark on a young Zulu computer programmer taking a weekend away from her sophisticated city life to return to her family's homeland for a traditional christening. This mingling of the old and new is perhaps the greatest intrigue that Africa has to offer.

CHAPTER 3

Textile Arts in Africa

by Kaye England, 1999. 47″ × 57″
(119 cm × 145 cm).

Embroidery is a needlecraft technique
used all across Africa to create a design
on fabric. Based on that concept, panels
of animals were created on a home
sewing machine utilizing its embroidery
capacity and then made into the center of
six "Variable Star" blocks. African-
themed fabrics were used throughout the
quilt, and special thought was put into
the sashings and borders. Note that the
outside stars in the sashing have points of
unequal length, and a star is quilted into
the center of each with red thread. Also,
masks, in the same shape as the leaves,
have been cut from a printed fabric to
anchor the corners of the vine and
provide a witty and whimsical note.

A Rich and Ancient Textile Tradition

The world's most ancient textile comes from Egypt, in the north-
eastern corner of Africa. Its light and gauzy weave, made with the
finest threads, testifies to a sophisticated textile industry at least five
thousand years old. Even in Nigeria, where the climate is much more
humid than in Egypt and therefore more destructive to textiles, traces
of loom-woven plant fibers at least one thousand years old have been
found. Records show that early Mediterranean sailors learned that, in
addition to the North African corn they routinely traded for, African
fabrics found lucrative markets in Greece and Rome. When the
Portuguese began trading with West Africa in the fifteenth century,
they returned home with fine raffia cloths and mats from the Kongo,
which they valued as highly as any other artifact they obtained.

All this is by way of saying that there has always been, in sub-
Saharan, as well as in North Africa, a tradition of textiles. Muslims
swathe themselves in fabric from top to toe as a sign of modesty.
Even where people practice animist traditions and partial nudity is not
uncommon, there are well-established textile traditions. Some
traditions have more in common with basketry than with traditional
cloth-making practices, but then textiles in Africa have always, in
different places at different times, served as far more than simply a
material for clothing. Textiles have been used as a medium of
exchange, as medicine and magic totems, as a link between
generations, and as a sign of social rank.

There are hidden meanings in many designs of African fabrics.
Because African fabrics are produced primarily for local markets, the
designs may represent local proverbs or a person's stature in society. (If
a fabric is to be exported, other patterns are chosen.) Therefore, the
wearer of a certain fabric or piece of clothing conveys a specific

message to the remainder of the group. Some patterns are reserved for royalty, priests, elders, or other important personages of the clan.

The Fabrics of Africa

Kente Cloth

Kente cloth is perhaps the most widely known textile of Africa. It is now completely identified with the Ashanti of Ghana, although the word comes from a neighboring group, the Fante. Kente cloth is made of strips woven by men on special narrow looms. The strips are interlaced to form a length of fabric that men wear as a sort of toga over the left shoulder and upper arm. Women generally wear two smaller lengths, one as a skirt and the other as a bodice. Myths link the making of kente cloth to the spider, nature's own weaver, and weaving the cloth is fraught with superstition: no work is begun or ended on Fridays, and any major mistake demands an offering to the loom.

Kente cloth was originally made of white cotton with a bit of indigo patterning, but it changed when silk cloths from Europe became available through Portuguese traders. The silk fabrics were

Here's a uniquely African take on a portable sewing machine! The wheel at the side with the handle indicates that it is a hand-powered model. Equally popular are foot-powered treadle machines, which some manufacturers still produce especially for the African market. Tailors and seamstresses often work in the open-air markets that are found throughout the temperate and equatorial zones of the continent. Photograph copyright © Jose Azel/Aurora.

COLORS AND DYES

Color is symbolic, but the meaning afforded each color varies with different groups. To the Ashanti, black is the color of the ancestors, and of night, the time of most spiritual power. However, to the Kongo, black is identified with the land of the living, because it is the color of the fireplace, where the family gathers. To them, white represents the power of the ancestors and the spirit world. Red is perhaps the one color that means pretty much the same thing in most African cultures: it is the color of blood and danger and so it comes to mean the deadly power of the king and *voudou* or sorcery.

Most of the dyes used in African textiles are still produced from natural materials. The most common dye used in Africa is indigo, which is extracted through great effort and an advanced technical knowledge from a plant. Indigo, as every quilter knows, yields a wonderful range of blues, from nearly black to the palest of sky-blues. Brown is obtained from cola nuts and other trees and plants, as are red and black. Mud and clay are also used to produce some colors. The effect of mordants is well known, and such knowledge is essential for the production of certain shades of red, especially on wool and leather.

Madder, a plant-based dye, is being used to create a brilliant hue at a commercial dye yard in Fez, one of the ancient cities of Morocco. Great earthen vats are built on site. Each section is meant for a specific solution. Photograph copyright © Nathan Benn/National Geographic Image Collection.

carefully unraveled and their thread rewoven into the fabulous designs favored by the Africans.[1] Later, silk was imported in skeins, and throughout the nineteenth century kente cloth for Ashanti kings was enormously costly, since it was made exclusively of the imported fiber. Historically, only the Ashanti of Ghana and the Ivory Coast used silk in their textiles.

The colors of kente cloth have particular meanings: yellow stands for wealth or royalty; white is for goodness or victory; black means death or old age; red symbolizes anger or violence; blue is for love; green represents energy or new growth; and grey is for shame or blame. Even when we know the key to the colors, it is not possible to understand fully the message that the weaver was transmitting with his choices.

Although kente cloth today is likely to be made of rayon, very little about its production has changed. Primitive wooden looms are operated by hand; dyes come from plants or mud and are made up either in large calabashes or in clay dye vats built on the ground. Designs continue to be restricted, and each new pattern is offered first to the king. If he declines it, the pattern may still be produced and sold to ordinary persons: even today, in the beginning of the twenty-first century, it is unthinkable that a commoner would wear the same design as the king of the Ashanti.

ADINKRA SYMBOLS

Each adinkra symbol has a name and a definite meaning, which does not always seem related to the name.

 Head seen from the back, which stands for valor, bravery, and courage.

Five tufts of hair evoke the traditional hairstyle of priestesses.

A chain means "We are bound in life as in death."

 This talisman against negative influences is a good luck charm.

 A windmill means the ability to face difficulty in life.

 Eagle claws allude to the hairstyle of the Queen Mother's servants, and its meaning is the ability to serve.

Ram's horns mean humility, excellence, wisdom, and knowledge.

 A four-story house or castle stands for government, authority, or the seat of power.

 The highest adinkra symbol, a bull's-eye, or three concentric circles, stands for authority, grandeur, firmness, and magnamity.

Adinkra Cloth

Another cloth originally set aside for the exclusive use of royalty, adinkra cloth communicates through symbols. Although it is now identified with the Ashanti of Ghana, it is said to have come into their kingdom as a spoil of war; along with the fabric came the method of stamping the bark-dye designs. The fabric was seized in an 1818 battle from a king named Adinkra, who, when he was taken prisoner, wore a cloth with symbols that conveyed his sorrow at the deaths of his soldiers and the loss of the battle. The designs found on adinkra fabrics were originally worn only by royalty and spiritual leaders for mourning during a funeral service. In the language of the Ashanti, *adinkra* means "saying good-bye to one another." Adinkra designs serve two purposes: they convey a message, and they enhance the beauty of the fabric.

The symbols in adinkra cloth remind people of proverbs and ideas that have special meanings, such as unity, patience, and fearlessness. A chief on a mission of peace might wear clothing printed with the *binkabi* symbol, which stands for unity. The symbols themselves are very decorative, and twelve are shown on the quilt "Adinkra Symbols" on page 70.

The patterns found on raffia pile fabrics are the same ones found on wood carvings, in house decoration, body markings, and other Kuba work. Although all the patterns are named, those bearing the same name are not necessarily identical, and different names are applied to the same pattern. Sounds very much like quilts, doesn't it? From the collection of Kaye England.

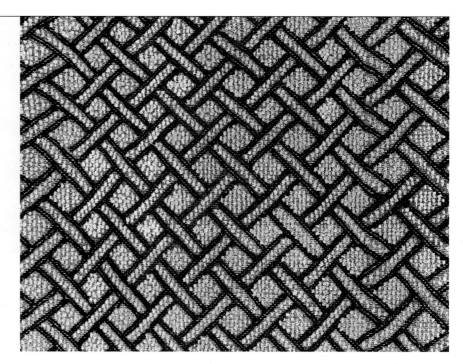

Raffia Fabrics

Raffia is a natural plant material used in clothmaking, especially in the Democratic Republic of Congo (Zaire). The technique of extracting long threads from the leaves of the raffia palm has been known among the Kuba (a subgroup of the Kongo) for centuries, and a tradition of fine fabrics that closely resemble velvets, satins, taffetas, and damasks has developed from this basic material. Their beauty was well known in Europe, described at the beginning of the eighteenth century by Father Laurent de Lucques: "The fabrics of these regions . . . are truly beautiful. . . . Some of them closely resemble velvet, others are so richly adorned with various decorations and arabesques that it is a wonder that anyone working with leaves . . . could make such fine and beautiful fabrics, which are every bit as good as silk."[2]

Seven species of raffia palms grow in Africa, and the largest of them can grow to 30 feet (9 m) tall. The leaves of this giant can be as long as 50 feet (15 m) when stretched out flat, making them the longest leaves of any plant on earth today. The raffia fiber is extracted from the young leaves, in many fairly simple, but time-consuming procedures. At one stage, the raffia fibers are bundled into skeins, which are often sold for export; it is very likely that they find their way to our local craft and florist shops, where we buy strands for such uses as tying packages.

If the raffia fibers are to be woven into fabric, they are split, sometimes with the fingers, but often with a comb that cuts the fiber into threadlike widths. Some cultures on Madagascar have learned to

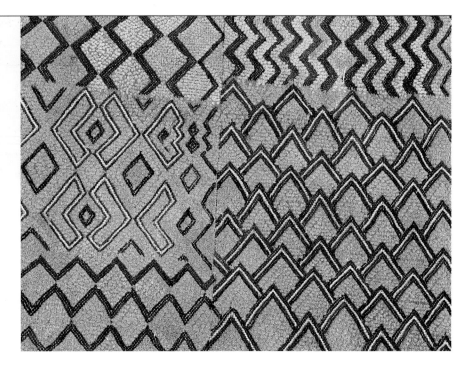

The designs are worked freehand onto the background fabric, from a repertoire that contains thousands of motifs. One study reports that of all geometric patterns possible in design, two-thirds are found in Kuba textiles. From the collection of Kaye England.

twist the ends of raffia threads together to make a continuous length for weaving, but this technique has not developed elsewhere. Most often, the woven textiles are limited to the length of the thread as it comes from the palm leaf. The exception is southeast Nigeria, where fiber lengths are knotted together so that the material can be woven exactly like cotton.

The value of these fabrics cannot be overestimated; Kongo kings were once prohibited from wearing any other fabric, particularly imported ones. Raffia textiles served as a form of currency and a means of paying taxes. Legends tell of kings crossing rivers on raffia mats, and no marriage or funeral can take place without many such mats. Although we have no proof of anyone rafting a river on a raffia mat, they are waterproof and lightweight, as well as beautiful. Embroidery gave the soft, textured appearance Europeans admired like velvet.

Kuba tradition holds that their legendary ruler of the seventeenth century, Shamba Bolongongo, traveled west from his country (at the mouth of the Congo River) to learn weaving and embroidery, then brought these arts back to his people.[3] Both techniques are required for the production of the renowned "Kasai velvet," which is made completely of raffia. In their original context, the finished rectangles of fabric were used for clothing and furnishings for people with high status, but as they made their way to Europe and America, they became highly collectible objets d'art. The artists Paul Klee and Henri Matisse hung their Kasai velvets on their studio walls so they might enjoy the complex geometric patterns. (Another artist, Pablo Picasso, was said to have been greatly inspired by African art, particularly masks, just before he began his Cubist period; he later denied having ever seen African art of any kind.)

The highly prized velvets are painstakingly tufted by hand by women, although the weaving of the ground cloth is done by men. The pile is created by millions of tiny stitches taken through the warp of plain-weave fabric. Each stitch is cut so that two tails of equal length extend from the surface of the fabric. These are never more than one-eighth-inch (0.3 cm) long. The exacting stitching and clipping continues until each area of the design is covered in the desired color. A variety of colors may be used for the tufting, and it can be different from the ground cloth, portions of which may be left untufted as part of the design. Red, yellow, black, and white constitute the usual colors of Kuba textiles. When the tufting work is completed, it is fluffed up by passing the hand back and forth across the stitches many times.

Bark Cloth

Ordinary people—those not of the ruling class—generally used materials such as bark cloth for their garments. Because it is made of readily available natural materials, bark cloth is far cheaper than any other type of fabric. And because it is visually so different, it made the distinction between social classes quite pronounced. Bark cloth is made, as its name would indicate, from trees, with the layer just underneath the rough outer bark serving as the raw material. In many cultures, the outer bark is tied back around the trunk of the tree to protect the cut area and to stimulate the growth of a new crop.

The tender bark is cut into long strips, soaked in water, then pounded with a mallet for hours until the fibers are compacted together enough to retain their shape, a process similar to making felt or paper. The piece is then dried in the shade. In the Pygmy and Mangbetu social orders, the work up to this stage is done by the men, then the women decorate the cloth.

Mud Cloth

An African fabric that has been very popular in the European and American market since the mid-1980s is bogolanfini, or mud cloth, from Mali. According to African textile scholar Duncan Clark, mud cloth was elevated from the fabric of the disenfranchised, the poor and lowly, to a symbol of national identity when a Malian designer, Chris Seydou, who worked in Paris, used a length of it in his 1979 runway show. He quickly garnered the support of wealthy customers from his home country and continued to feature the fabric in his lines through the 1980s and into the 1990s, until his early death in 1994. Later, he helped to set up factories to produce manufactured copies of traditional mud cloth designs. The availability of the fabric meant that manufacturers of sheets, towels, and other home furnishings could incorporate the distinctive black-and-white designs for their lines, and the garment industry enthusiastically imitated Seydou's original, and expensive, designs.[4] Mud cloth is widely available in the United States, in machine-printed interpretations, as well as in the traditional hand-worked version, which can be identified by the seams that bind narrow fabric strips into a width of a suitable size for clothing and home furnishings.

The fascinating aspect of this truly indigenous African fabric is the technique of using mud as dye. During the dry season, when the ponds of Bamana, near the capital of Mali, begin to dry up, mud is removed from the very center, the deepest part. Stored in a covered container for a year, the mud ferments and turns a deep black. A portion is dipped out of the container and diluted a bit with water, then painted onto plain white fabric (in the aforementioned narrow strips) that has been dyed yellow with a solution obtained from leaves. The tannic acid in the leaf solution makes iron oxide in the mud colorfast. Mud cloth designs are predominantly black, requiring that most of the fabric be painted. After two or more coats of the mud dye have been applied, the open areas of the design are bleached to white.

Although there are said to be four traditional colors in which Mali mud cloth can be worked—black, grey, red, and white—black is by far the most common. Some mud cloth currently being produced arranges abstract motifs in geometric patterns using three colors, such as black, white, and yellow. Individual motifs seem to be widely recognized in

Although we might not always know it when we see it, mud cloth, or machine imitations of it, has been widely available in the United States for some time. From the collection of Mary Elizabeth Johnson.

Modern manufacturing methods make replicas of traditional hand-printed and hand-woven African fabrics available for quilters. This selection, purchased at a quilt festival in the United States in 1999, includes two versions of kente cloth, two imitation Indonesian wax-resist prints, and one brocade with a design based on a raffia fabric. All are manufactured in Africa. From the collection of Mary Elizabeth Johnson.

Mali, and often have names that describe the pattern, such as "fish bones" or "little stars." Other motifs refer to historical events, and others to aspects of women's daily experience, such as being co-wives and the rivalry within polygamous households, although writer Duncan Clark warns against trying to read a cloth literally to form a coherent text. The fabrics are merely reminders of traditions.[5]

Wax-Resist Prints

More direct are the messages sent on some wax-resist prints, and we are reminded of early quilters and the way they used their work to

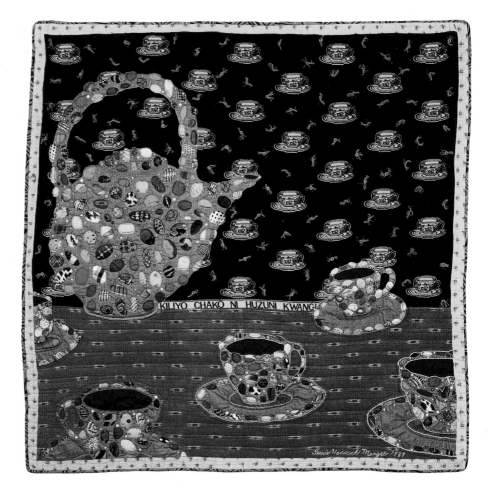

▶ STONE TEAPOT

by Terrie Mangat, 1987.

46″ × 46″. (117 cm × 117 cm).
An African "fancy print" featuring
teacups and a Swahili message that
means "Your pain is my sorrow,"
inspired this original and witty
response.

express their feelings or to send messages. Reports Duncan Clark,
who wrote the following in 1997:

> In the last few years, several researchers have noted that
> women have been able to use the imagery and associated proverbs
> of some wax-print cloths to send messages they would otherwise be
> unable to express publicly. As yet it is unclear how widespread this
> practice may be, but it certainly adds a new dimension to some
> familiar designs. Susan Domowitz noted that among the Anyi of
> Côte D'Ivoire, the tensions underlying the apparent harmony of a
> polygamous household were expressed by a cloth featuring circular
> designs. The cloth was known as "co-wife rivalry is like cow
> dung," a proverb which ends "the top is dry but the inside is
> sticky." The familiar spider designs are associated with the
> warning proverb "what one does to the small harmless spider, one
> does not do to the big dangerous one." A woman who was tired of
> her husband's unfaithfulness could let him know by wearing a
> cloth featuring a bird flying from the open door of a cage. The
> name of this design is "You go out, I go out!" Another one bears
> the equally blunt title, "condolences to my husband's mistress."[6]

This avenue of expression is open to women through fabrics that began as traditional wax-resist, like Indonesian batiks but have evolved into the machine-printed fabrics known as "fancy prints." Today's fabrics are far from the originals, which were created by hand-applying wax to the fabric in patterns designed for many colors. After industrialization, resin was substituted for wax, but the fine cobweb of lines that identified fabrics printed by the wax method was retained. Now, although the fabrics are entirely roller-printed, the fine network of cracks is often in the design. And because there is an active and competitive fabric-printing industry in Ghana and other sub-Saharan countries, it is possible for the consumer to order custom designs. Direct-printing methods can achieve fine detail, and even photographs can be printed onto fabrics.

Imported fancy prints, as well as many other African fabrics, are widely available in the United States. Vendors who specialize in such cloth are beginning to appear at quilt shows around the country. It is satisfying indeed to browse a booth filled with African fabric samples and recognize kente cloth, bologanfini, adinkra, and the other styles that have sprung from African designs.

Asafo Appliqué

Appliqué is a technique that has long been known to the peoples of Africa. The ancient Tuareg appliquéd their tents with leather and the nomadic Berbers applied narrow wool patches to their tents, not only to repair holes, but to execute motifs that brought good luck and prosperity to those who passed through the tent's opening. However, appliqué as practiced by the Fante of Ghana and the neighboring Fon

One of the most common Asafo flag images is that of an elephant with its trunk coiled around a palm tree. The palm tree is considered the strongest tree and is a symbol for eternity; the elephant, of course, is an icon of strength. If an "elephant" company uses this motif, the proverb being illustrated is "Only the elephant can pull down the palm tree"; if a "palm" company uses it, the meaning is "Even the elephant cannot uproot the palm tree." Silk appliqué flag from the British Museum.

of Dahomey (now the Republic of Benin) is the most familiar to the rest of the world. Their imaginative and widely known flags, banners, fabulous tunics and other clothes speak directly to a quilter's sensibilities.

The A'safo are the warrior class of the Fante and use the appliquéd flags to identify military companies. The first recorded instance of an Asafo flag dates from 1693, when an English trader on the Gold Coast chronicled seeing an Asafo general flying a flag "white with a black man brandishing a scymitar,"[7] but it is fairly certain that the flags were already well established. The Asafo were no doubt influenced by the military pageantry and accoutrements of the European detachments that had been visiting their shores for some two hundred years, and it is believed that they adopted the idea of "flying the colors" from those Portuguese, French, and English soldiers.

Asafo flags usually measure about three by five feet (90 cm × 150 cm) and are made of cotton fabric, although wool felt and silk have been used. One side of each flag is a mirror image of the other, which results in numbers, if they are used, being reversed on one side. (The numbers identify the company.) Most flags are finished with a patchwork border of squares, triangles, and rectangles, and a final flourish of white fringe. The field of each flag illustrates a particular proverb, a device for teaching the company's history to new recruits. Proverbs are closely associated with oral history by the Fante and other groups who had no written language. The proverbs are chosen to send a specific message about the company or to speak of its power and glory, usually at the expense of some rival. The messages once became so incendiary that a governing body was formed to oversee future designs to ensure that no group would be so insulted that they would declare war.

Although much of the imagery of the Asafo flags is

Banners are still being made by the Fon, especially for the ready market of travelers who appreciate their lively shapes and primary colors. Their similarity to United States folk art appliqué strikes a warm response in most of us, although they were designed to intimidate their adversaries. From the collection of Kaye England.

A royal war tunic from the Republic of Benin contains much symbolism in its appliquéd and embroidered details. The rings embroidered with chain stitch on the yoke indicate the rank of the wearer, who was probably a king, since red is a royal color. The appliquéd triangles represent the leopard, another royal symbol. Late nineteenth century, Musée de l'Homme, Paris.

military in nature—"No one can defeat us but God"—much of it is also instructive. "The monkey leaps only as far as it can reach" not only warns potential adversaries not to try anything foolish, but instructs children to "Look before you leap." Particularly interesting are the flags that use images from European technology to intimidate enemies: "The train is always ready to go" means that the company is prepared for all comers; another is "Like the airplane, we can go anywhere." Images of religious deities are common, as might be expected, and animals of great strength are favorite motifs. Peter Adler and Nicholas Barnard point out in their book about the flags of the Asafo that the lion, being a creature of the savanna, is not native to the woodlands of the Fante, and its frequent appearance on Fante flags is directly attributable to British influence, because it is the English "quintessential visual metaphor for power."[8]

Fon Appliqué

Dahomey, now the Republic of Benin (part of the ancient, fabulously wealthy, and enormous kingdom of Benin), is separated from Ghana by the relatively small country of Togo. The Fon people of Dahomey developed an appliqué tradition of their own, and early on established a special guild of appliqué artists who worked exclusively for the court. The country was ruled by kings from about 1700 to 1892, when it was colonized by the French, and the court appliqué artisans during that time mainly illustrated power and strength—for example, in battle scenes, executions, and portrayals of the king as a powerful animal. Vast festival tents and banners, which depicted scenes of heroic victories in war, as well as abstractly embellished umbrellas and war tunics, were designed and stitched according to the desires of the king. Most special court drapery was intended for the annual war waged against a neighboring country to take prisoners to be sold into the lucrative slave trade.

The appliqué traditions of the Fon changed after colonization by the French and again when the country gained its independence in 1960. Traditional symbols lost their meaning, and these days only the oldest appliqué artists are able to interpret them. Many of the appliquéd flags and banners being produced now are intended for the tourist market and thus feature motifs that sell well.

Masquerade Costumes

Without question, some of the most impressive examples of needlework to be found in Africa are the full-body masquerade costumes worn on special festival occasions by various ethnic groups. Among the Chokwe of central Africa, the arms, legs, and trunks of the performer are encased in a colorful crocheted or hand-looped bodysuit. No two of the crocheted suits appear to be the same. There are, of course, stripes, as well as lozenges, diamonds, and squares worked in all manner of color combinations. Over the bodysuit go skirts, scarves or neck ruffs, masks, and headdresses. The choice and combination of these items depend on which spirit is being impersonated. Sometimes it is an ancestor, sometimes a nature spirit. Imposing masks, made from bark cloth, carved wood, fiber, feathers, and/or more crochet complete the effect.

The Ibo of Nigeria wear costumes to represent spirits, some of which are obviously good, benevolent beings, while others are the threatening powers that also influence their lives. The red Ibo costume

shown on these pages is meant to demonstrate the power of beauty, because it represents a comely maiden spirit, but other costumes are made of horns, smelly medicines, and animal skins to portray the dark, heavy side of the spirit world. Field researchers working for the British Museum have noticed that in parts of Iboland a skilled tailoring guild has begun to emerge to meet the demand for masquerade costumes.

Both the Ibo and the Chokwe feature female spirits prominently in certain of their ceremonies, but the masqueraders are men. The female ancestor or spirit is represented by a full-body costume with attached conical shapes

The ideals of feminine beauty are represented in this mask from the Chokwe peoples of the Democratic Republic of Congo. The mask is the finishing touch to a full-body masquerade costume. The elegance of a celebrated female ancestor is represented by the elaborate coiffure, which is crocheted from cotton yarn to represent the mud-packed wigs that were favored by Chokwe women until the 1950s. The National Museum of African Art, Washington D.C. Photograph by Franco Khoury.

representing breasts. The breasts may be crocheted on Chokwe suits, but they are often of carved wood in other cultures. Most African cultures afford equal status to women, acknowledging them as nurturers to the young, equal providers of food, and full partners in life's tasks. However, no matter how graceful, beautiful, or accomplished she might be, a woman reaches her potential only in motherhood, according to most societies. Initiation rites for young women prepare her for motherhood; initiation rites for young men honor not only the male novice but his mother, who is seen as a fulfilled woman because she has reared her son to adulthood. Maskers play the part of the fulfilled woman ancestor or other spirits in the entertainments that accompany these initiation ceremonies.

Full-body masking keeps the identity of the wearer a secret while he or she portrays as convincingly as possible the character the costume represents. In most societies, the men who mask belong to organizations with strict and uncompromising initiation rituals; members are more or less understood to be custodians of that particular order and its secrets. Masking is a serious undertaking, done for a purpose. The masks themselves are considered to be either the representatives of certain specific spirits or the spirits themselves. They are kept out of sight unless they are in use, as are the costumes.

No matter what spirit or ancestor is being represented, whether benevolent or beastly, the sight of one of these figures completely masked from top to toe is impressive indeed, even to observers who have become rather blasé in the face of twenty-first-century technology.

This full-body costume from the Ibo of Nigeria is five feet, nine inches (175 cm) tall, and would have been worn with a tall wig or headdress of fiber and cloth. Of particular interest to quilters are the needlecraft techniques, including couching, french knots (which delineate the chin), and intricate cotton appliqué. From the Eric D. Robertson Collection, The Center for African Art, New York.

Quilting and Patchwork in Africa

It will hardly come as a surprise that there is not much of a quilting tradition in Africa, because so much of the continent is covered either by desert or by steamy rainforest, and there is little need for the warmth that quilts provide. The one place that quilting is used to make warm clothing is among the Berbers of Morocco, who spend part of the year in the cold mountain regions with their sheep; shepherds sometimes wear quilted cloaks made of several layers of fabric. Neither has much patchwork developed, although there are examples of raffia fabric blocks set together in a light-and-dark checkerboard pattern to make a larger width of material for a long skirt. Similarly, fragments of bark cloth have been pieced then pounded together to make a bigger piece, but in no particular pattern.

However, there is one stunning and unique application of quilting and patchwork: the incredible sets of horse armor that originated among the desert warriors of the southern Sahara. The riders of the horses also wear quilted armor, but their suits are not nearly so intricately pieced nor as decorative as those of their horses. In African armor, the quilted material itself protects against arrows and other weapons, unlike the quilted undershirts that Europeans wore underneath the armor of the Middle Ages, which primarily cushioned them against the abrasive, cold metal.

The tradition of quilted armor developed in an area of the southern Saharan region that extends as far east as Khartoum, Ethiopia, where the White and the Blue Nile meet, and as far west as the middle Niger plain, around Lake Chad. The armor protected the precious cavalry horses of the kingdoms in western Sudan. These kingdoms, which flourished from about the eighth to the late nineteenth century, were always in conflict—sometimes for territory, sometimes for the control of trade routes, and sometimes for religious

What could be more thrilling to a quilter than a glimpse of a ceremonial procession such as this one in Niger, with its display of colorful quilted armor on horses and on soldiers? Photograph copyright © Photo Researchers.

reasons. Because they do not breed easily in central Africa, horses had to be imported from the ports of West and East Africa, across the Sahara, to the center of the country. Neither were they immune to the tsetse fly, as are the native animals. The difficulty of obtaining and maintaining the horses made them extremely valuable and great care was taken with them.

To make the horse armor, cotton cloth, originally hand-woven and hand-colored, was cut and sewn into patterns instantly recognizable to quilters as traditional patchwork designs like "Flying Geese" and "Windmill." The patchwork fabric was cut into shapes that fit over a saddle and hung nearly to the horse's feet; there was also a neck wrap that covered the horse's chest. Some suits of quilted armor included a shield for the horse's head. Several layers of fabric were put together, and the innermost layer, the lining, was sometimes a beautiful print. Decorative quilting stitches held the multiple layers together.

Although modern weapons have made it obsolete, horse armor is still an integral part of ceremonial processions and parades. Replicas of traditional sets of armor are made as needed so that military companies can always turn themselves out in grand traditional style. (For more information, see the two quilts inspired by sets of horse armor: "Fulani Stars," page 94, and "Sky Serpents," page 122.)

Embellishment

Embellishment is essential to the African character. Even when making the most rudimentary tool for everyday use, the African craftsman decorated with a design. And, as Laure Meyer points out in her book, *Art and Craft in Africa,*

> *Regardless of the living standards of their inhabitants, whether modest or regal, [African] dwellings displayed, and still display, the same concern for aesthetic beauty. Each object they made—be it a chair, a bowl, a weapon, or a fabric—reveals the artisans' particular care to create an appearance that pleased the eye. . . . The craftsmen were not content to produce a functional object, it also had to be beautiful: to satisfy their pride as craftsmen, to please their client, and, of course, to attract future business. The results were very often nothing short of remarkable, considering the limited means at their disposal.*[9]

As we have discussed, the object first had to fulfill its purpose. However, after that consideration was taken care of, the craftsman was free to make it beautiful. And they did so with great enthusiasm and ingenuity. Every craft developed ornamental techniques that added only to the appearance of the product. In making fabrics, gold, silver, or even tin was added to fabric weaves. The metallic yarn would be wrapped around the fiber yarn before weaving, an example of embellishment at a most basic level.

As quilters, we know that appliqué, patchwork, and embroidery are, in their essence, methods for creating a design on or with fabric to suit the artist—they are ways to embellish the fabric. So too is fabric printing, which is, of course, more direct but usually requires technical knowledge not easily obtained by a layperson. However, African artisans carved gourds to print on fabric; there are also examples of drawing and stenciling on fabric. Another method for applying design to fabric is embroidery, which has been employed to fabulous effect in Africa.

Especially outstanding is Hausa embroidery, which uses gold- and silver-wrapped threads for the most luxurious work and provides an African source for our quilting in metallic threads. They also use ordinary hand-spun cotton and wild silk. For the most part, Hausa embroidery is carried out by men working on men's clothing, although women started embroidering in the 1970s, working in a different style from the men. They apply their work to household items, such as pillowcases and bedcovers, as well as to garments.

Charms

The business of appliqué does not stop with the application of one piece of woven fabric to another. As we will see, the custom of attaching amulets to war shirts anticipates our practice of embellishing quilts with beads, charms, buttons, and other decorative items. African textile experts John Picton and John Mack have found that many materials other than fabric were appliquéd. Quilters will find their definition of the technique interesting:

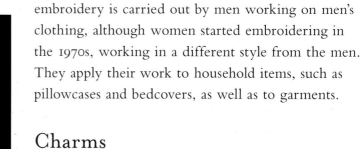

This war tunic and helmet are from the Akan of Ghana. Amulets for protection and luck were wrapped in leather cases and attached. Brass bells, horn, fur, cowrie and other shells, as well as beads and reptile skin, are stitched to the base fabric. Each item has special magical powers. From the Eric D. Roberston Collection, The Center for African Art, New York.

Appliqué is the word used to describe the process of adding further materials to an already-woven textile base. Normally the term is applied to the laying on of additional pieces of textile, but we also . . . include such supplementary materials as beads and shells, metals and jewelry, animal fur and bundles of medicine. Taken in this broad sense, the technique can be seen to be well established throughout Africa: ceremonial cloths, banners and flags are often appliquéd; so too are cloths incorporating magical substances and the skins with beadwork decoration of eastern and southern Africa. The technique is certainly indigenous in Africa.[10]

A fascinating application of this three-dimensional appliqué is found in the "charm gowns" made by the Hausa of northern Nigeria, although it is only one of two decorative techniques used on the

▶ Tribal March

by Laurie Barnett, 1999. 36″ × 50″ (91 cm × 127 cm).

In the true spirit of African embellishment, the quilter selected the warrior motif from the border fabric and enlarged it for her center block, then added buttons, beads, and feathers for three-dimensional detail. (The dancing warrior design comes from a rock painting in the Sahara.) Dynamic golden spikes in each corner, accomplished through foundation paper piecing, further enhance the quilt.

Africa is rich in textiles. This handwoven length of Kuba cloth from the Democratic Republic of Congo is intricately stitched with faggotting and other open-work embroidery. From the collection of Kaye England.

fabric. The Koran, the holy book of the Muslim faith, is incorporated in three different ways: first, verses are written on paper, which is folded and placed in leather pouches that are then appliquéd to the garment; second, verses are written in ink or vegetable dye all over the garment, with particular emphasis on the back, thought to be the most vulnerable area; and, third, the garment is washed in water that has been used to clean boards on which the Koran was written. Customers may order these charm gowns from tailors, and they wear them to ensure good luck and to protect them from harm.

War shirts from the Ashanti of Ghana are similar to charm gowns; they protect against bad luck or injury in battle. On war shirts, the Koranic verses often appear with animal claws and teeth or magical herbs, all enclosed in protective packets of leather, then appliquéd to the garment. One can only imagine how heavy these shirts became as more and more charm packets were attached; they would in effect become a suit of armor, as they would be impervious to all but the luckiest hit by an arrow. However, the physical aspect of the shirt seems not to have been valued; it was the spiritual.

To Learn More About African Textile Traditions

This overview has presented only a sampling of the many textile traditions of Africa; it is limited to those kinds of fabric that we judged to be of particular interest to quilters. There is much more to be found in independent study. Reading about only the weaving techniques employed in different areas of the continent could keep you absorbed for days.

Specific garments offer many possibilities for study and for inspiration for quilt designs. Ceremonial skirts in some groups are made of long panels of cloth that wrap around the body; a decorative motif might suggest a block design for a quilt. The gowns and pants favored by Muslim men are very full and loose and are often made of

Here's an idea for transporting your fabric stash. This woman will offer her fancy prints for sale in an outdoor market, still common all over Africa. The range of designs she offers is amazing, but if the customer can't find what she wants in this selection, she can go to a fabric house and order a design of her choosing and/or invention. Photograph copyright © Cary S. Wolinsky/Trillium Studios.

wonderfully striped fabric overlaid with all manner of appliqué and embroidery. Skirts and capes from ceremonies of initiation into adulthood for the Maasai and the Ndebele provide ideas for color schemes and repetition of motifs. The regalia worn by the officials during special ceremonies can be intriguing; for example, one group cloaks the priests in a scarlet costume that represents the pangolin, or scaly anteater, a most remarkable creature. The costume is quite beautiful, with its layers of scalloped red felt that reach to the ankles.

The history of textile production in Africa is rich with impressive examples of advanced technology that did not damage the environment, used renewable resources, and provided lovely results. Many of these intriguing methods are still being used and are well worth independent study.

CHAPTER 4

Drawn with the Same Brush

ZIMBABWE ZEBRAS

by Kaye England, 1997. 31″ × 36″
(79 cm × 91 cm).

Eight small patchwork blocks mingle
seamlessly with appliquéd African motifs.
Lush plant forms around the edges of the
central medallion soften the transition
between the panel and the borders.
Embellishment is essential to the success
of "Zimbabwe Zebras." Crystal beads of
irregular size simulate pebbles at the edge
of the pool; a button stands in for a
coconut in the palm tree. The zebras'
manes are three-dimensional, a
wonderful effect of raw-edge appliqué.

African Designs Have Familiar Feeling

As you begin your exploration of African sources of design, you will
often thrill with recognition to discover the similarity between many
traditional African designs and familiar quilt patterns. You will find
pinwheels, autograph blocks, stars, and many other motifs that have for
centuries been part of African design and for two hundred or more
years have been used in American quilts. You are certain to have a
new perspective on how to integrate these well-known motifs into
your quilt designs. You will see unique ways of grouping or repeating
a familiar figure; you will get new ideas about how to space a single
motif on a surface; and you'll find great ideas for color schemes.

Africa enjoys a marvelously rich repertoire of geometric designs,
which has evolved in part because the Muslim faith forbids the
reproduction of animals or humans. In place of realistic
representations, fanciful arabesques and swirls have
joined with precisely partitioned squares and rectangles.
In this trove may be found innumerable designs
appropriate for patchwork. However, it is not just the
Muslim influence that has produced so many geometric
designs. As we have seen, the Ndebele prefer angular
designs because they work easily in the grid system of

This beautifully made nineteenth-century mask represents
Everywoman to the Kongo. Black and white triangles signify
hearthstones and domesticity, and the diagonal lines are tears,
resulting from the hardships of a woman's life. Photograph
copyright © Peabody Museum, Harvard University. Photograph
by Hillel Burger. Image #17-41-50/B1908.

51

Esther Mahlango working on a wide, colorful panel with typical geometric shapes. Photograph copyright © Carol Beckwith/Angela Fisher/Robert Estall Photo Library.

beadwork; they also choose them for their house murals. As we learned in the discussion of Kasai velvets, two-thirds of all geometric patterns possible in design are found in Kuba textiles, again because the embroidery was worked on an interlocking grid of threads.

Cultures that are thousands of miles apart use the same motifs. Many reasons can be put forth for this, such as that one culture acquired the motif from another through an item that was traded, but probably the motifs evolved within each culture according to what they were meant to represent. The inevitable conclusion is that the same motifs developed independently in many cultures, more or less simultaneously.

Same Symbol, Different Meaning

Every symbol is freighted with significance in each culture, but the meanings vary from culture to culture. We know that the four-triangle block is a symbol of masculinity to the Zulu, but that in the adinkra symbolism of the Ashanti, it means strength in adversity. Practically all of the most common geometric patterns mean different things to different cultures.

In Cameroon, half-square triangles represent a crocodile's back; in the Democratic Republic of Congo (Zaire),

A war shield from the Songye in the Democratic Republic of Congo (Zaire) displays the four-triangle block. This design is found again and again in African art and seems to be used particularly when black and white are the only colors of dye or paint available. Photograph copyright © The Barbier-Mueller Museum, Geneva. Photograph by P.-A. Ferrazzini

ASHANTI PEEL

Although it is highly possible that every motif found in African decoration has a meaning unknown to us, we can still appreciate and enjoy it. In some cases, when a motif belongs to both African design and American quilt patterns, our idea of what the motif stands for may preclude any willingness to think about the African meaning. We have allegiances to our own folklore.

Such is the case with the motif that quilters know as "Orange Peel," a circular design that consists of four elongated ovals arranged around a shape known in the quilt world as a "reel." Quilt lore says that the reel design was adapted from the spool used to wind rope and wire; the spool had squared ends with elongated corners and was a familiar sight at the seaports when

An ancient bronze urn from Ghana contained a motif known to quilters as "Orange Peel."

immigrants came to America. It is thought that quilters first saw it there and integrated it into their patchwork. It forms the basis of many familiar quilt designs, such as "Oak Leaf and Reel" and "Double Wedding Ring"; it also shows up in many very early floral designs as the center of a flower.

With such history accompanying the quilt design, what are we to make of it when we see it on an Ashanti bronze urn that was worked long before America was discovered? The only answer is, of course, that the design truly is no more than a study in how to partition a circle, and different people came up with the idea at different times. Whatever its meaning was to the African who incised it into the pot she created makes no difference. We can have our folklore and she can have hers.

◀ ASHANTI PEEL
by Terri Gunn, 1999. 32″ × 39″ (81 cm × 99 cm). The fabric choices of this quilt suggest the detail incorporated into much of the metalwork of the Ashanti. Two richly colored fabrics, deliberately chosen for low contrast, were used to execute the "Orange Peel" design with an African flair.

where the Kongo live, these triangles suggest hearthstones and domesticity. The basic nine-patch design is known by the Hausa of the southern Sahara as "five houses"; the same design refers to a turtle in the Cameroon grasslands. The turtle in the Hausa design vocabulary is symbolized by a pair of ovals interlocked as in a chain.

One of the most basic motifs in African ornamentation is a four-triangle block, the result of drawing diagonal lines through the center of a square from corner to corner. See "Fulani Stars" (page 94) for a photograph of this motif applied to horse armor. It also enhances "Zulu Vista" (page 106).

As you explore the art of Africa, you will discover the world of symbols, which are thought-provoking and instill a respect for the process that reduced a complex pattern to a cleanly polished graphic design. A good example of this is the representation of a leopard's pelt with isosceles triangles, as practiced by Cameroon artists. The

▶ INCADE YE MPHILO
by Sandy Heminger, 1991. 52″ × 68″ (132 cm × 173 cm).

Africa had a subtle, but very definite, influence in this color scheme. The tawny gold background suggests a lion's pelt or a stretch of savanna, and earth is found in the ochre and deep gold tones, which, as in nature, are contrasted with touches of cool blue from sky and water. In the words of the quilter, "Before Christianity came to the Zulu tribe, their Bible was the *Incade Ye Mphilo,* which translates into English as the 'Book of Life.' Colors have significance in the Zulu culture, and certain colors signify privileges within the group. Darker colors are worn by older members, and brighter colors are reserved for childhood and symbolize a carefree spirit. The 'Tree of Life' block seemed to carry with it the most significance for this quilt. It was the last block I made, and I tried to use an example of all the fabrics so that the leaves on the tree were symbolic of the life in the other 11 blocks, given to them by the color of the fabric."

impression is clearly of a light-and-dark overall pattern that repeats motifs of the same size throughout the design; a leopard's coat is just that. There are many other examples, each of which can impress you with the depth of study behind them and their applicability to quilt design.

What Makes a Quilt Seem African?

Africa was a source of inspiration to the great innovative artists of the early twentieth century, such as Pablo Picasso, Henri Matisse, Romare Bearden, and Paul Klee. They drew new forms and devised vibrant color combinations from the arts of Africa. Fashion designers of today, such as Donna Karan and John Galliano, have looked to Africa for design ideas. Yet we do not label the work of any of these creative people as particularly African. They take what they see and apply their own creativity to it, producing their own unique product. The lesson that we can learn from them is that of the process one goes through between inspiration and interpretation.

In discussing the common motifs shared by African art and quilt design, the underlying suggestion is, of course, that any of these motifs can inspire a quilter, and the interpretation is easily accomplished when the quilt is a fairly direct reproduction of the inspiration. Truly, the direct reproduction of a specific motif may be the easiest route to interpreting an inspiration, but it is not always the most satisfying. Good design results from deeper thought and more

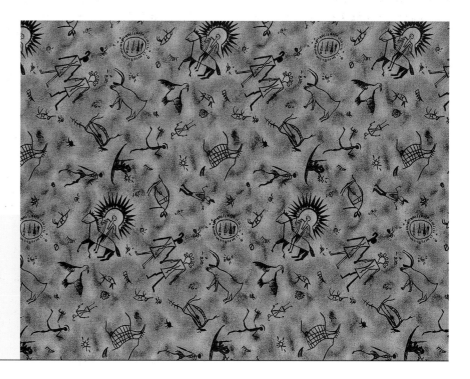

The design of this fabric, which was produced in four different colors, came directly from a Bushman rock painting from the Tsibab ravine in southwest Africa. Fabric designed by Kaye England for South Sea Imports.

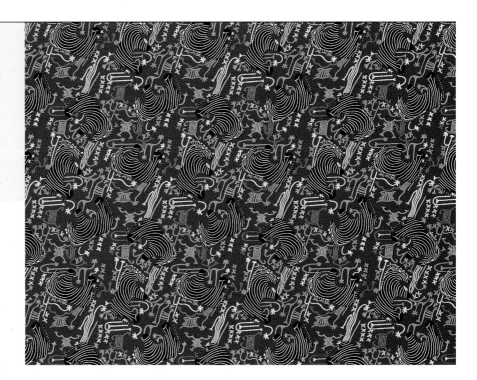

Another print inspired by a carved soapstone zebra from Zimbabwe, Rhodesia. The background colors for prints such as these have been carefully chosen to coordinate with fabrics that would be selected for an African-themed quilt. Fabric design by Kaye England for South Sea Imports

A quilt from the third quarter of the nineteenth century, "Callie Lu's Sunflower" *(left, top)*, is done in the traditional fabrics from that period. The color scheme is familiar, and that familiarity is reassuring but maybe just the tiniest bit too comfortable. When "Callie Lu Goes to Africa" *(left, bottom),* the mood changes. The deeper colors and the exotic quality of the prints make us give this favorite old pattern a closer look. Are we sure these are sunflowers? Maybe they're some thrilling new specimen, something we've never seen before.

innovative ideas than the mere copying of a motif. There are other, more subtle, ways to incorporate an African inspiration into a quilt.

Let's look at color. When all is said and done, color keeps us quilting—we love it and we love to play with it. It is also the most direct way of interpreting an inspiration. You can approach a design with the goal of planning a color scheme that will speak to your design inspiration. Perhaps you're struck by images of northwest Africa, on the Mediterranean coast. Your color scheme would have to include deep blue, to represent the water, dusky reds for the Moroccan textile tradition, perhaps off-white for the tracery of carved screening used in the architecture, and deep black-green for the palm trees in this environment; primary colors in shades that give the impression you're after. Say that your love is the savannas, the grasslands. You would work in a golden palette, moving from deep saturated colors to sands, beiges, pale browns, and whites, with the gentlest of greens suggesting the growth that nourishes those amazing herds of animals. Speaking of animals, your grassland would hardly be complete without some animal images executed in raw-edge appliqué. To move from inspiration to implementation, you must examine your source and analyze the colors that create the mood that enchants you.

Fabric choices are part of color selection, but when the fabric is a print, it can become an even more powerful component to the quilt. We as quilters are most fortunate that a number of fabric manufacturers offer lines with African themes. Not only have the fabric designers already researched the colors that will help us to achieve an African feeling in our work, they have studied the motifs that tell an African story. These motifs are often drawn directly from an African source.

The advantages of African-themed fabrics are many, but chief among them is that you can choose a favorite quilt pattern, build a color scheme in these fabrics, and presto! you have a traditional quilt with an interesting new depth. The two examples on pages 56 and 57 handsomely illustrate these advantages.

◀ AFRICAN LOG CABIN

by Anita Gwin, 1998. 60″ × 60″ (150 cm × 150 cm).

A traditional "Log Cabin" block is arranged in the "Barn Raising" version, with a beautiful bordered central medallion. The light fabrics represent the shifting dunes of the desert and the dark fabrics, the jungle. The reds and purples speak of bougainvilla and orchids and other tropical blooms. All the colorful, printed fabrics are from the African line of one manufacturer, South Seas Imports, and were designed by Kaye England.

As color and pattern are essential to moving a design from inspiration to interpretation, so is the way a motif is repeated. The repetition of the motif creates the movement in the piece. In some quilts, you will choose a regular repetition of the motif, primarily because you have created a sense of movement with the color scheme—see "Ibo Walls" (page 83) for a good example. In other instances, you will move a motif around all over the place, but keep your colors constant—see "Woman Warrior" (page 144). Sometimes you will pick out one extraordinary motif and make it the center of interest, so that everything else in the quilt is secondary, no matter how interesting those elements are in themselves—"Woman Warrior"

▶ FRIENDSHIP SAMPLER

by Peggy McKinney, 1999. 50″ × 72″ (127 cm × 183 cm).

This quilt is composed primarily of blocks made by members of a quilting group. Although many African-themed fabrics were used in each block, the black background and the clever set make the piece seem truly "African." Notice how the "Ibo Walls" block (page 82) has been used both as a border element and as a strip down the middle of the quilt. The detail highlights the appealing appliqué depicting the women warriors of Africa.

▲ AFRICA SCRAP MANIA

by Kaye England, 1998. 74″ × 84″
(188 cm × 213 cm).

In an experiment to Africanize a quilt
block whose motif may not have come
directly from African designs, 45 different
patchwork patterns were worked up in
African-themed fabrics. Whether airy or
earthy, or a combination of the two, the
resulting color schemes speak to an
African origin. Taken together (with one
prized silk-screened mask block from
Africa in the mix), the blocks applaud the
application of a new way of thinking to
that which is familiar—this is not your
grandmother's sampler quilt!

and "Life Is Not What You Expect" (pages 144 and 150). Very often
the original object that inspired you will lead you toward a plan for
repetition of the motif.

Always remember that the credo of African art is that form
follows function. Every object is made to fulfill a purpose. When you
make a quilt, it must fulfill whatever function you intend it for,
whether it is to keep you warm, beautify a place of worship, tell
someone you love him or her, provide comfort, or fill a place in your
heart. It won't be African if it doesn't do what you need it to do.

Part Two

A CARAVAN OF
QUILTS

All but one of the quilt projects that follow are the work of one designer, Kaye England, whose fascination with Africa continues. The inspiration she draws from her research into all things African is unending. You will undoubtedly have the same experience—the more you look, the more you will find.

The quilts show you how to go from an inspiration to an interpretation in fabric. They capture a feeling or essence of Africa. The sense of the desert may be interpreted in sandy, earthy colors and undulating curves, with perhaps a tiny touch of teal to represent the occasional oasis. A woven basket can be represented by a simple shape repeated in two colors. We see these as lessons in how to move from an idea to an actual quilt, and we hope that you will be encouraged to try your own experiments. You're sure to find some happy surprises along the way.

If you wish to duplicate the quilts shown here, directions have been included for each project. Each technique is described with the first project in which it is used. Check page 62 for a complete listing of all step-by-step techniques. Kaye chose the techniques she used in the following quilts for their ease of execution. Her techniques, while fast, do not sacrifice quality. We believe in clean work, done to the best of one's ability. However, we also believe in doing the best you can and moving on. We also believe in handwork, especially when it is the best way to achieve an effect. Machine work is great and Kaye does a lot on the machine, but there's something very satisfying about quilting a piece by hand to get the texture you want. Besides, embellishing, which is mostly done by hand, is such a joy! It's just so much fun to pick out special areas of a quilt to emphasize with metallic quilting, couching, or beads or sequins.

We invite you to try the methods that accompany the quilts and see if they don't save you lots of time. However, if you are committed to your own special way of working and don't want to change, that's fine too. Just pick up that needle and stitch your way to Africa!

Kenya Four-Patch

TECHNIQUES—A QUICK REFERENCE

Each of the following techniques is discussed in detail with the directions for the quilts in which it first appears.

Adinkra Symbols

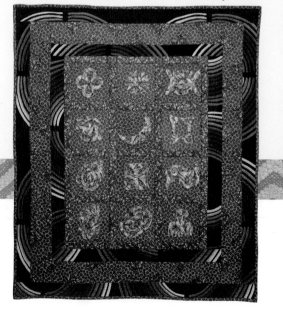

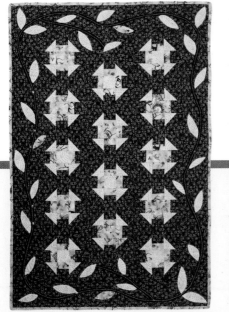

Yoruba Dash

Fulani Stars

Sky Serpents

Bushongo Magic

Woman Warrior

GoGo and the Veil of Rashaida

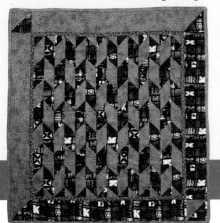

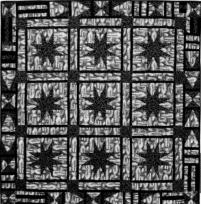

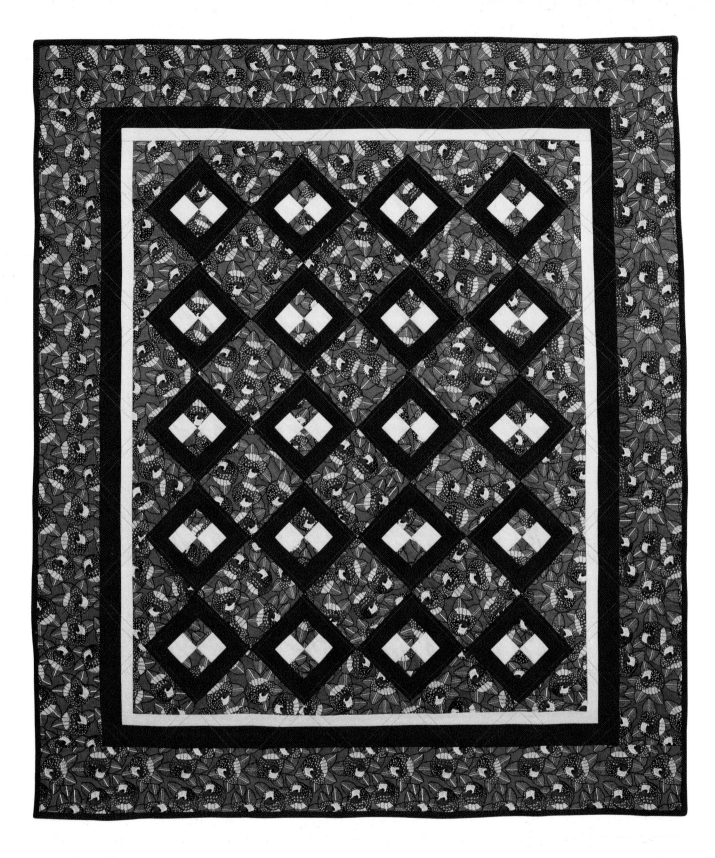

He who does not know one thing knows another.
—Kenyan proverb

Kenya Four-Patch

◀ KENYA FOUR-PATCH
by Kaye England, 1998. 47″ × 54″
(119 cm × 137 cm).

Vibrant colors and bold prints bring an African feeling to the traditional block in "Kenya Four-Patch." The quilt would be at home in almost any decorating scheme; while lively, the color scheme is not strident or overpowering. The traditional four-patch has long been used to teach children to piece; it is still a good starting place for the beginning quilter. In this design, the basic patch has been enhanced with a border on each block.

Much about Kenya seems familiar: the name of its capital city, Nairobi; its national language, Swahili; its largest native ethnic group, the Kikuyu; and its world-famed game parks. One of the most stable and prosperous countries in east Africa, Kenya is bounded by the Indian Ocean, Somalia, Ethiopia, Sudan, Uganda, and Tanzania. It has always been attractive to visitors, whether they were early Indian traders, British colonialists, or modern tourists.

A great deal of Kenya's appeal is in its stunning physical geography. Although it lies squarely on the equator, the mountains that make up much of the country provide a cooling altitude; Mount Kenya is the second-highest peak on the continent. Additionally, the Great Rift Valley, with its fertile volcanic soil, runs from Lake Rudolph in the northern part of the country to Lake Victoria in the

Tsavo National Park, in the Great Rift Valley, is the largest of Kenya's many game reserves, where tourists may view and photograph the abundant wildlife; hunting and trophy-taking were outlawed years ago. This terrain is known as a thornbush plain, and the vegetation, though scrubby, provides sustenance for the herds of animals that call it home. Each species of grazing animal eats a different plant. The zebras like something different from the antelope, who eat something the water buffalo doesn't want, and so on. Thus nature has provided for all. Photograph copyright © Brian Boyd/Colorific!

southeastern corner. The valley, traditional home of the Kikuyu, is a place of rushing streams, rich soil, and abundant plant life. The Maasai have long shared this area with the Kikuyu, moving their cattle about in a time-honored seasonal grazing plan.

The richness of Kenyan natural resources provided the inspiration for "Kenya Four-Patch." The point of departure is an exotic, leafy print with a deep brown background that suggests the shade and shadows of the deep forest; the dashes of red and yellow make us think of the plumage of quick-moving birds, sensed, yet not wholly seen, as they flicker and dart through the foliage. Yellow and a tiny print that gives a rust-red appearance have been selected as accent colors, adding a hint, perhaps, of the desert that borders the lush forest in the lowlands of Kenya.

One important lesson to be taken from this quilt, in addition to the special techniques, is that three, and only three, carefully selected fabrics are used to create a dynamic, lively version of the traditional four-patch pattern so familiar to quilters.

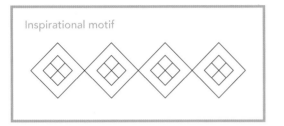

Inspirational motif

Layout diagram

Making Kenya Four-Patch

FABRIC REQUIREMENTS

Based on 42" to 44" (106 cm to 112 cm) selvage to selvage

Leafy print fabric	1½ yd (140 cm)
Solid yellow	½ yd (45 cm)
Tiny print in rust-red	⅔ yd (60 cm)
Backing fabric	2¾ yd (250 cm)
Binding fabric	½ yd (45 cm)

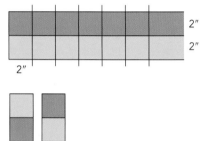

2"
2"
2"

Step 2

Step 3

Quick Piecing the Bordered Four-Patch

1. Cut two strips of yellow and two strips of leafy print fabric measuring 2" × 40" (5 cm × 106 cm). Right sides together, stitch together along one long side, using a ¼" (0.75 cm) seam allowance. Press seam allowance to darker fabric. Repeat with other two strips of fabric.

2. Use rotary equipment to square one end of this strip set and then trim off segments in 2" (5 cm) increments. Cut 40 segments. Join two segments, rotating one so that contrasting fabrics are opposite each other. Press. Make 20 four-patch units, each one 3½" × 3½" (8.5 cm × 8.5 cm).

3. To border four-patch units, cut four strips of rust-red fabric measuring 1¾" × 40" (4.5 cm × 106 cm). Cut strips to length you need as you work with each four-patch unit. (There is no need to cut them into separate lengths before you begin.) Sew a rust-red strip to each side of a four-patch unit, cutting it the same length as unit. Then sew a rust-red strip across the top and bottom of each unit, making it same length as unit plus two border strips. Repeat until all 24 four-patch units are bordered.

TECHNIQUE

Chain sew one edge of several blocks to a 1¾" × 40" (4.5 cm × 106 cm) strip of rust-red fabric, leaving a little space between blocks. Cut blocks apart and press seam allowance to new strip. In same way, attach border to opposite sides of blocks. Square all four corners. Add border strips to remaining sides. Square again. Finished blocks measure 5½" × 5½" (14 cm × 14 cm).

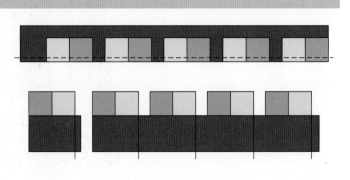

Diagonal Set

A diagonal set is sewn in rows, just as a straight set. The difference is that triangles rather than full blocks are sewn to row ends. When all rows are joined, bases of triangles meet to form straight sides.

4. Measure a pieced block along its diagonal and add 3″ (7.5 cm). Cut four squares with sides that length from leafy print fabric. To make triangles for sides, cut each square in half twice diagonally (this makes two extra triangles).

5. Add 2″ (5 cm) to block's diagonal length, and cut two squares that dimension from leafy print. Cut each square in half diagonally to make triangles for corners.

6. For plain blocks, cut twelve 6″ (14.5 cm) squares from leafy fabric. Side triangles and corner triangles are larger than necessary to give room for adjusting.

7. Turn layout diagram slightly on an angle so that rows are horizontal. Starting at top, row 1 contains one bordered four-patch block with outside triangles on either side. Label it and all following rows. On row 2, there are two bordered four-patch blocks separated by a plain block, with outside triangles on the ends. Row 3 has three bordered four-patch blocks, two plain blocks, and side triangles on ends. Rows 4 and 5 each have four bordered four-patch blocks, three plain blocks, a side triangle on one end, and a corner triangle on the other. Row 6 repeats row 3, row 7 repeats row 2, and row 8 repeats row 1.

8. Join blocks and side triangles in rows as indicated, pressing seams away from pieced block.

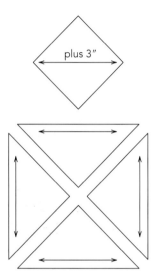

plus 3″

Step 4

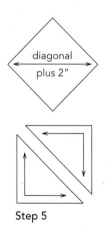

diagonal
plus 2″

Step 5

Step 8

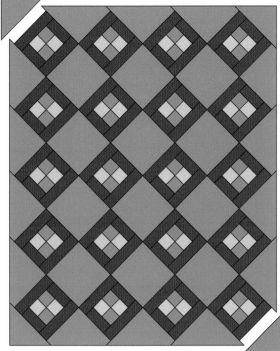

Step 9

9. Join rows, making sure rows 4 and 5 alternate so that corner triangles are in corners and side triangles are on sides. Join two remaining corner triangles.

10. When all blocks and triangles are joined and seams are pressed, decide how to trim edges. You can "float" center by leaving a margin around the outside, or you can obtain a sharp effect by trimming so that corner four-patch borders hit exactly at edge: be sure to allow ¼″ (0.75 cm) seam allowance or sharp corners will be chopped off when you join first border. Whichever look you choose, trim so that top and bottom edges of quilt are same width and both sides are same length.

Borders

11. To determine length of border strips for sides, measure along center line of quilt from top edge to bottom edge. To determine length of border strips for top and bottom, measure quilt along center line, after you have attached two side borders. Widths of border strips are as follows:

Yellow inside border	1¼″ (4.5 cm)
Rust-red inside border	2″ (5.5 cm)
Print outside border	5″ (14.5 cm)

When there are multiple borders, you should always determine length for each additional border by measuring after the previous one has been joined.

Quilting

12. To add batting and backing, see page 155. Pieced areas of the quilt are echo-quilted; that is, each shape is outlined with quilting stitches ¼″ (0.75 cm) from seamline. Setting blocks are quilted in a diagonal crosshatch design, with rows of stitching placed ¼″ (0.75 cm) apart, as are borders. See page 158 for instructions on binding quilt.

One falsehood spoils a thousand truths.
—Ashanti proverb

Adinkra Symbols

ADINKRA SYMBOLS
by Kaye England, 1999. 34″ × 40″
(85 cm × 100 cm).

The symbols chosen for the quilt were
selected for their visual appeal rather than
for the messages they send. However, it
is interesting to know what the designs
mean.

The Akan were ancestors of the present-day Ashanti, who
prospered through trade and agriculture. The center of their
kingdom has always been the ancient city of Kumasi, in the
highlands off the coastal plain of the Gulf of Guinea. During the late
seventeenth century, Kumasi was a great center of trade and of
political, religious, and intellectual life.

The Ashanti are noted for their belief that their dynasty was
established with Osei Tutu in 1701, when he claimed that a golden
stool fell out of the sky into his lap as a sign of his election to lead
the people. The golden stool became the symbol of the unity and
vitality of the kingdom. The concept of the golden stool has not
always been well understood by Europeans. In an attempt to conquer
the Ashanti during the colonization of
Ghana, one British governor sat himself
upon the stool to demonstrate his
authority. This gesture sparked a bloody
rebellion, because to the Ashanti the spirit
of their people abides within the stool, and
no one, not even the *Asantehene* (king),
actually sits on the golden stool.

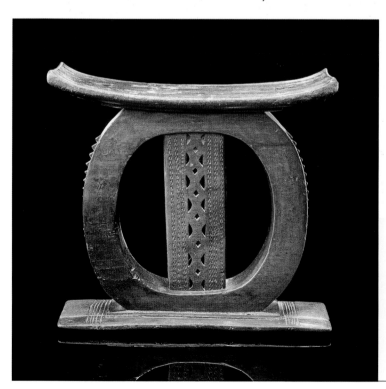

A wooden Ashanti stool from Ghana is typical
of those used by men as they gather to visit
and talk; the Golden Stool is similar in style,
but larger, and covered in gold leaf. Carvers in
Ghana still produce stools today. Photograph
copyright © Barbier-Mueller Museum,
Geneva. Photograph by P.-A. Ferrazzini.

No discussion of the Akan/Ashanti is complete without mentioning their abundant gold; Ghana was at one time known as the Gold Coast. There are a number of rich mines in the country, but Akan women continue to pan for gold in rivers and streams, using gourd containers to sift the gold-bearing sand. Much trading was done in gold, which was prized more highly by other cultures than by the Muslim Akan. Gold traders used brass figures, cast in the lost-wax process, as weights. Prized as collectibles today, many of these tiny figures were of beautifully detailed animal forms such as roosters, monkeys, or geese; numerous abstract designs were also made.

As one studies the art of the Akan/Ashanti with an eye to Adinkra symbols, one begins to see them in many other applications, not just on fabrics. We find them carved on stools and on brass gold weights. We see them worked into gold beads that were strung together and hung in doorways to signify the wealth of the household. We begin to understand that they convey a message wherever they are used. In fact, their original function was to decorate funerary cloths, an appropriate application, for *Adinkra* means "saying good-bye to one another when parting."

Layout diagram

The sophisticated symbols apparent in the arts of the Adinkra are but one indication that the Akan were some of the most cultivated people in ancient Africa. The meanings of the symbols in the quilt are as follows.

Upper left corner: Humility and servitude (*kuntin kantan*)

Top row, center: The chief (*asantehene*)

Upper right corner: Sun rays, the double crescent moon, and the Ashanti stool: the universe (*kojo baiden*)

Second row, left: Immortality of God (*gye nyame*)

Second row, center: The moon; all the positive female qualities, such as love and kindness (*osrane*)

Second row, right: The home; security and peace (*fihankra*)

Third row, left: The ancestor of water spirits (*snake*)

Third row, center: Piety and good fortune—wards off evil (*keerapa*)

Third row, right: Courage and determination (*gyamu*)

Bottom row, left: Unity and harmony—wards off conflicts (*binkabi*)

Bottom row, center: The seal of law and order—the powers of the court (*mmra krado*)

Bottom right corner: The wooden comb—the positive qualities of women, such as patience and care

Making Adinkra Symbols

Raw-Edge Appliqué; Quick Sashing

FABRIC REQUIREMENTS

Based on 42" to 44" (106 cm to 112 cm) selvage to selvage

Fabric A—Light background gold for symbols	½ yd (45 cm)
Fabric B—Medium value gold print for sashing and middle border	½ yd (45 cm)
Fabric C—Medium to dark turquoise/blue print for background of symbols, corner squares in sashing, and middle border	¾ yd (70 cm)
Fabric D—Dark large geometric print for inside and outside borders	⅔ yd (60 cm)
Backing	1 yd (90 cm)
Binding	⅓ yd (30 cm)

Raw-Edge Appliqué

1. Cut out each of 12 symbols using templates on pages 165–169. Finish raw edges by sewing along each cut edge with a small zigzag machine stitch.

2. Cut 12 squares of fabric C, each measuring 6" (15.5 cm). Pin each symbol in place on a background square, centering it horizontally and vertically. Straight-stitch or zigzag symbols onto background around all cut edges of appliqué, as shown. Raw edges will become more and more textured over the life of the quilt, adding visual interest.

Step 2

Quick Sashing

Although sashing appears to be long rows of fabric that join long rows of blocks, with squares at the corners of each block, in our method we actually attach sashing to individual blocks first, then sew blocks (with sashing) together in rows, and, finally, sew rows together. Here's how.

3. Cut 31 rectangles of fabric B, measuring 1½" × 6" (4 cm × 15.5 cm). Cut 20 squares of fabric C that measure 1½" × 1½" (4 cm × 4 cm).

4. Arrange appliquéd squares in desired order, with four rows containing three blocks each. Join a rectangle of sashing to *left* side only of left-hand and center blocks of first row and to *left* and *right* sides of right-hand block. Now join these three blocks to each other with sashing between blocks. Repeat for all four rows.

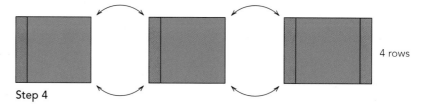

Step 4   4 rows

5. To make crosswise rows of sashing, you will need four corner blocks and three sashing rectangles for each row. Sew a corner block to the left side of two rectangles, and then to left and right sides of third rectangle. Join three units together so that squares alternate with rectangles. Repeat five times.

Step 5   5 rows

6. Alternate rows of blocks and rows of sashing, finishing with a row of sashing at top and bottom. Match up seams in sashing and blocks. Stitch. Check photo of finished quilt to be sure sashing is correct.

Piecing Middle Border

Step 7

7. To make connectors, cut 40 squares of fabric C 3½″ × 3½″ (9 cm × 9 cm). Cut 80 squares of fabric B 2″ × 2″ (5 cm × 5 cm).

8. Use two gold connectors on each turquoise square. Place a gold square face down on opposite corners, aligning raw edges. Stitch diagonally across, through the exact center of each connector as shown, from corner to corner. Fold the gold square over along the seam. Press little gold triangle up to match edges of the turquoise square. Trim away inside half of connector. This piece is now a square, and if you leave turquoise fabric intact, it is much less likely to get out of square. Make 40 squares, 10 for each side of quilt.

Step 8

9. Join two rows of 10 squares for sides. Then join two rows of 10 for top and bottom of quilt, taking care to turn corners correctly. Check photograph to be sure rows are right.

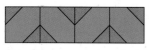

Step 9

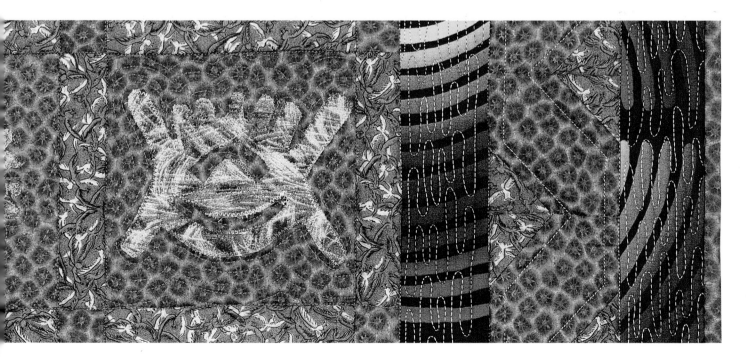

TECHNIQUE

It is best to piece the zigzag border before cutting the inside border, just in case you need to make some adjustment to the measurements to make it fit your pieced border. You can always cut the strips a little longer or a little shorter, a little wider or a little narrower in order to match the exact length of your pieced border, which can't be adjusted.

Step 11

Plain Borders

10. For inside border, cut two strips for sides 2¼″ × 27½″ (5.5 cm × 70 cm). Cut two strips for top and bottom 2″ × 24½″ (4.75 cm × 61.5 cm). For outside border, cut two strips for sides 2½″ × 36½″ (6.5 cm × 91.5 cm). Cut two strips for top and bottom 2½″ × 34½″ (6.5 cm × 86.5 cm).

11. Join both sides of inside border to quilt top. Then join top and bottom pieces. Corners are not mitered. To join pieced borders, join sides first, then top and bottom. Be careful placing pieces, so design will turn the corners exactly right.

12. Join outer border in place, sides first, then top and bottom. See photograph of finished quilt.

Quilting

13. To add batting and backing, see page 155. Each symbol is echo-quilted, in lines ¼″ (0.75 cm) apart, until background square is filled. Zigzag border is stitched ¼″ (0.75 cm) on each side of every seam, following shape of piece. Both geometric borders are machine quilted with a variegated rayon thread in a meandering stitch. For binding, a dark turquoise print was chosen to finish the quilt. It matches the background of the symbols and the zigzag border, creating an impression of a whole cloth to which pieces have been added, much in the manner of African appliqué. See page 158 for instructions for applying a binding.

A proverb is the horse of conversation: when the conversation lags, a proverb will revive it.

—Yoruba proverb

Yoruba Dash

◀ **YORUBA DASH**
by Kaye England, 1998. 35″ × 50″
(89 cm × 125 cm).

A brown and wine print with scrolling black lines contrasts with the fresh, tender green of the "Churn Dash" blocks, sending a message of new growth underscored by the leafy, climbing vine of the border. One advantage of this design, wonderful for the beginner, is that you don't cut any triangles! Even though triangles appear in the final design, they are actually squares folded over, called connectors.

The work of the Yoruba, past and present, inspired three quilts presented with this pattern. All are based on the traditional American "Churn Dash" pattern that has been a favorite of quilters for two hundred years. The goal is to demonstrate how a familiar pattern can be given a feeling of Africa through astute choice of fabrics.

A dance skirt from Nigeria displays some of the favorite colors and patterns chosen by the Yoruba for their beadwork. Although used primarily for ceremonies, the skirt is thought to attract lovers and enhance the desirability of the wearer. From the collection of Becky Hancock.

It is generally recognized that the Yoruba kingdom of Oyo, located in what is now Benin, had one of the most brilliant cultures of all the early African states. Its influence stretched along the Gulf of Guinea from Lagos in Nigeria through the coastal regions of Benin and Togo by the time the Portuguese traders arrived in the fifteenth century. Generally known as Yorubaland, the empire reached its height in the eighteenth century and continued in influence until its political structure was crushed by a combination of the Fon armies of Dahomey and the unrelenting attacks of the fierce Fulani Muslims in the early nineteenth century.

The Yoruba social system centered on city life: the eleventh-century city of Oyo was defended by a 20-foot wall that circled 25 miles around it. Inside were elaborate palaces, courtyards, and dwellings. Benin City, to the southwest, was also a splendid city, governed by a thoughtful ruler, who actively recruited sculptors and other artists, as well as specialists in medicine, diviners, men of religion, military men, and legal administrators. The city sparkled with

AFRICAN DASH

by Laurie Keller, 1998. 48″ × 68″
(122 cm × 173 cm). Quilted by
Melissa Taylor.

Some viewers see stars; others see exotic
flowers blooming on the dark background
of this scrap quilt. Although each motif
is made from only one fabric, clever
template positioning gives a different
impression. No fabric has been used more
than once. Some fabrics, although by no
means all, contain overtly African motifs;
the spirit of the quilt comes from the
vivid and bold use of colored blocks set
into a dark background.

professionals and talented people from the kingdom. A third city, the
Ile of Ife, was the holy city of the Yoruba, because there, they
believed, the creator descended from heaven on an iron chain and
established the Yoruba kingdom. These were only three of the many
walled towns of the Yoruba, which still exist in some rural areas.

Like the Ibo, the Yoruba earned their living by farming and
working wood, stone, terra cotta, iron, copper, bronze, lead, brass,
and ivory. Whether made for religious or decorative purposes, the
quality of art from the Yoruba, and most especially that from Benin,
is among the finest to be found on the continent.

Making Yoruba Dash

FABRIC REQUIREMENTS

Based on 42″ to 44″ (106 cm to 112 cm) selvage to selvage

Light green print A for pieced blocks and leaves	½ yd (45 cm)
Light green print B for pieced blocks and leaves	½ yd (45 cm)
Dark, small-figured print for background	1½ yd (140 cm)
Solid dark fabric or bias tape for trunk of vine	½ yd (45 cm)
Backing fabric	1½ yd (140 cm)
Binding fabric	½ yd (45 cm)

Cutting

Layout diagram

Cut as follows. All measurements include seam allowances.

Light green print A

For the connectors, cut 56 squares
2½″ × 2½″ (6.5 cm × 6.5 cm)

For the centers, cut 14 squares
2½″ × 2½″ (6.5 cm × 6.5 cm)

2 small leaves

Light green print B

For the bars that join the "triangles,"
cut 56 rectangles
1½″ × 2½″ (4 cm × 6.5 cm)

6 large leaves, 20 medium leaves, and 3 small leaves

Dark, small-figured print for background

Cut 32 squares	2½″ × 2½″ (6.5 cm × 6.5 cm)
Cut 8 squares	3½″ × 3½″ (9 cm × 9 cm)
Cut 22 rectangles	3½″ × 6½″ (9 cm × 16.5 cm)
Cut 11 rectangles	2½″ × 4½″ (6.5 cm × 11.5 cm)
Cut 4 rectangles	3½″ × 7½″ (9 cm × 19 cm)
Cut 2 rectangles	2½″ × 6½″ (6.5 cm × 16.5 cm)

▶ A Dash on the Beach

by Susan Raban, 1999. 50″ × 62″
(127 cm × 157 cm).

What a difference a light background makes! One is tempted to think of the colorful stalls of an open marketplace underneath a bright African sun. This quilt is done in a "strippy" set and looks like a colorful African banner; the white background makes the colors gleam like tropical fruits in an ivory bowl. Some of the churn dashes are made with African-style fabric; mud cloth and kente cloth are easily recognized.

TECHNIQUE

This pattern can be sewn using the traditional way of piecing the "Churn Dash," but it is much easier if you work with connectors. By utilizing connectors, you complete the entire quilt as you go. However, using connector blocks requires an entirely different—but much easier—way of looking at your quilt. Because you don't make pattern blocks, then background blocks, then place them together, you don't actually see your "Churn Dash" until the quilt is nearly finished. It is wise to diagram on graph paper every quilt you piece so that you can easily figure out new ways of assembling familiar designs.

Making Churn Dash Blocks with Connectors

1. Study layout diagram to see how connectors are put together into units. There are four different units, and you will need a different number of each. Each unit is made up of rectangles and what appear to be triangles; those triangles are connectors, and they start out as 2½″ (6.5 cm) squares. All are cut from green print A.

2. Matching edges, place a green square face down in one corner of a 3½″ (9 cm) square of background fabric. Stitch diagonally across connector, from corner to corner. Trim inside corner of green triangle and press right side up to matches edges of dark square. The piece is now a square, and since background fabric is intact, it is much less likely to stretch out of shape. Make eight pieced squares for B units.

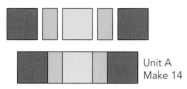

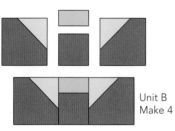

Unit A
Make 14

Step 5

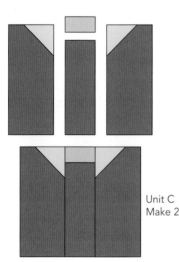

Unit B
Make 4

Step 6

Unit C
Make 2

Step 7

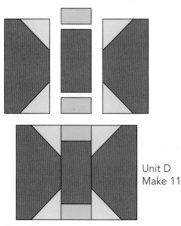

Unit D
Make 11

Step 8

3. Use same technique to join a 2½″ (6.5 cm) green square to upper right corner of a 3½″ × 7½″ (9 cm × 19 cm) dark rectangle. Join another square to upper left corner of a dark rectangle. Make another set of mirror-image pairs to use in C units.

4. Join a green square to upper and lower right edges of a 3½″ × 6½″ (9 cm × 16.5 cm) dark rectangle. Make 22 identical pieced rectangles to use in D units.

5. For A units, you will need two 2½″ (6.5 cm) background squares, two light green print B rectangles, and one light green print A square. Join to make a long strip. Make 14.

6. For B units, you will need two 3½″ (9 cm) background squares with a connector and a 2½″ (6.5 cm) background square attached to a light green print B rectangle. Join as shown. Make four.

7. For C units, take two mirror-image background rectangles with connectors and one 2½″ × 6½″ (6.5 cm × 16.5 cm) background rectangle attached to a light green print B rectangle. Join as shown. Make two.

8. For D units, take two background rectangles with two connectors and one background rectangle 2½″ × 4½″ (6.5 cm × 11.5 cm) with a light green print B rectangle attached to either end. Join as shown. Make 11.

Border

9. Cut two pieces of background fabric 6″ × 40½″ (15 cm × 101.5 cm) for side borders. Join to quilt. Cut two pieces 6″ × 33½″ (15 cm × 87 cm) for top and bottom borders.

10. To apply vine and leaves, cut a long bias strip in a suitable length for trunk of vine, and any branches you may desire. Pin vine in place around quilt border, creating curves and branches as suits your fancy. Using feather stitch or any fancy decorative machine stitch and contrasting thread, sew down center of vine to secure it to quilt top, leaving edges to fray.

11. Place leaves as desired around edges of quilt and raw-edge appliqué them in place (see instructions on page 73).

Quilting and Embellishments

12. To add batting and backing, see page 155. Center of each "Yoruba Dash" block is quilted in concentric circles. Leaves and vines of border are outlined to highlight shapes. Background is machine quilted in a free-motion design. See page 158 for instructions for applying a binding.

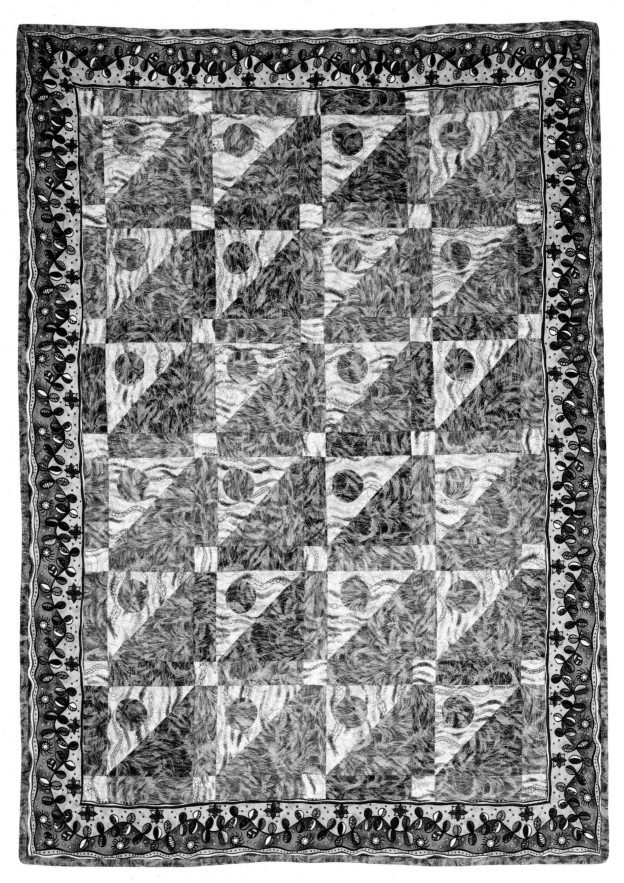

Fine words do not produce food.

—Nigerian proverb

Ibo Walls

◀ IBO WALLS

by Kaye England, 1998. 37½″ × 51½″ (95 cm × 131 cm).

This quilt incorporates a unique idea of cutting away the surface fabric to reveal another fabric beneath—an updated reverse appliqué technique. The building block is made in three colors: orange, brown, and green. The direction of the snake print is random throughout the quilt. In some blocks, it is horizontal; in others, it is vertical. The border pattern consists of a curving, leafy vine that divides the design into a light half and a dark half. One thinks of hills and valleys, or views above water and underwater. The corners are mitered so the pattern is uninterrupted.

This quilt design is taken from a design painted on a building and uses a simple square, triangle, and circle. The block is very easy to construct, using connectors for piecing and the raw-edge technique for appliqué.

I boland has been continuously inhabited by the Ibo for at least 5,000 years. Archaeological digs indicate that the Ibo were farming (cultivating yams) before 1,000 B.C., and blacksmithing before 500 B.C. The Ibo produced beautifully worked swords, hoes, axes, razors, bolts, and hinges, which helped them establish a lucrative trade with their neighbors. Pottery shards excavated from 4,500 years ago are very similar to pottery still being produced by the Ibo.

Their skill with iron also made the Ibo desirable as slaves. From the early sixteenth century through the next 300 years, first Portuguese, then Dutch and English, slave traders carried off nearly half a million people from Iboland. Even after the slave trade among

A slaver driving a woman to a slave-trade castle on the Ghanian coast is depicted on this Ibo dance headdress—the top hat of the man identifies him as a European. Photograph copyright © American Museum of Natural History/ Photo: E. Sackler.

▶ IBO SQUARED

by Judy Pleiss, 1998. 58″ × 74″ (147 cm × 188 cm).

This quilt groups four motifs into a block, then sashes them with bright purple—or is the sashing the black print? The circles are fused on top of the triangles, rather than reverse appliquéd, which gives a different effect. They are smaller than in "Ibo Walls."

Inspirational motif

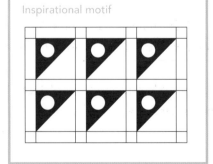

the Europeans declined in the 1800s, it continued among Ibo merchants, who prospered by selling not only the neighboring Yoruba but other Ibo as well.

Iboland is in the southeastern corner of present-day Nigeria, on the western coast of Africa, near the equator. (The country was, in 1967, declared by the Ibo military governor to be the independent Republic of Biafra, but has since, following a terrible civil war, been reintegrated into Nigeria.) It lies in a tropical plain between two rivers, with lushly forested areas flanking the rivers. The forests give way to grassland in the north. Villages are carefully planned, with broad streets. Buildings are made of clay with either thatched or tin roofs. The houses, painted in bright patterns of red, yellow, and black, were traditonally occupied separately by men or women, but now it is more customary for families to live together.

Making Ibo Walls

Two Ways to Make Circles

FABRIC REQUIREMENTS

Based on 42" to 44" (106 cm to 112 cm) selvage to selvage

Light print	¾ yd (70 cm)
Orange, brown, and green prints, each	½ yd each (45 cm)
Border fabric	1½ yd (140 cm)
Backing fabric	1½ yd (140 cm)
Binding fabric	½ yd (45 cm)

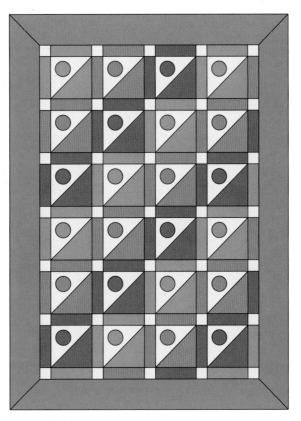

Layout diagram

Making the Blocks

Make 24 blocks, each measuring 6" × 6" (15.5 cm × 15.5 cm). Connectors are used to piece the blocks, and sashing is applied to each square as it is made.

1. Cut squares, each measuring 6" (15.5 cm) as follows: 24 of light fabric, 8 of brown fabric, 8 of green fabric, and 8 of orange fabric.

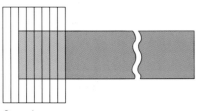

Step 1

Step 2

2. Place right side of a light square to right side of a dark square. Stitch through center of square on diagonal, from corner to corner.

3. Right sides up, press light fabric back onto itself so that half of square is dark and half is light. Cut away bottom layer of light triangle (layer between square and triangle).

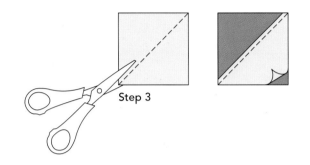

Step 3

TECHNIQUE

An alternative method for getting the circle into your design is to simply cut one out and fuse it down wherever you want it. It can be exciting to have the circles slightly off-kilter, not in exactly the same position on every triangle. Perfection is not necessary—it's better to have some fun!

Making the Circles

4. Make a circular template of plastic. Trace circle onto right side of light triangle. After opening a slit in center, it is easy to cut away fabric inside circle, either with a rotary cutter (slip a cutting board underneath!) or with scissors. Stitch around circumference of circle on the light fabric, close to the edge.

Sashing and Corner Blocks

5. To add sashing on each block, cut one 2″ (5.5 cm) square and two 2″ × 6″ (5.5 cm × 15.5 cm) rectangles matching block's dark fabric. Sew one rectangle to left side of block. Sew small square to end of other rectangle. Join unit to top of block.

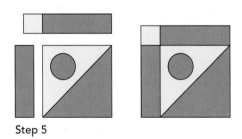

Step 5

6. Use photograph as a guide for placing colors; note that all three colors run diagonally across quilt. Add a square and a sashing strip to end of each row. Sew all six rows. Sew a strip of alternating sashing and corner blocks to bottom and right edges. Study photograph carefully to make sure color placement is correct.

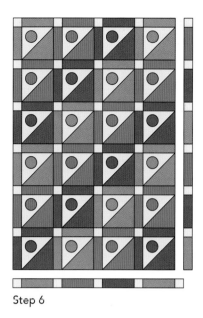

Step 6

7. Border fabric used to finish this quilt is printed with a design that is 4″ (10 cm) wide. Cut two strips 4½″ × 52″ (11.5 cm × 132 cm) for sides; two more strips 4½″ × 38″ (11.5 cm × 96 cm) for top and bottom. Center design so there is a ¼″ (0.75 cm) seam allowance on either side. Printed design on border will flow uninterrupted around corners if the corners are mitered. See page 155 for instructions for mitering a corner.

Quilting

8. To add batting and backing, see page 155. Varigated cotton thread was used to machine quilt "Ibo Walls" in a meandering pattern. See page 158 for instructions for applying a binding.

*We start as fools
and become
wise through
experience.*
—Tanzanian
proverb

Tanzania Tiles

by Kaye England, 1999. 30″ × 54″
(76 cm × 137 cm).

Although the block featured in this quilt is easily recognized as the familiar "Autograph Cross," the source for this quilt design was found on a plaited sisal mat from Zanzibar, Tanzania. The traditional autograph block takes on a completely different look with clever placement of color. A swirly multicolor print suggests the African sky at sunset. It is used for the background of the quilt, including the center of the "Autograph Cross" blocks, and for one border.

Zanzibar is an island in the Indian Ocean, off the east coast of Africa, known for producing spices, especially cloves. Its many cultural influences are reflected in its architecture: Muslim mosques, Hindu temples, Christian churches, and public buildings erected by Portuguese explorers, Omani sultans, and British colonial administrators. As one writer has said,

> Zanzibar is a place of strong sensations. It seduces the visitor with the scent of its tropical spices, the color of its flowers and fruits, the babble of different languages in the markets and the languid warmth of its equatorial sun. . . . Its cosmopolitan heritage is most evident in Zanzibar town, a charming if decaying port built of mortar and coral taken from nearby reefs. . . . The slave market . . . was closed in 1873 . . . and replaced by an Anglican cathedral.[1]

Children spread cloves out to dry on round plaited mats near Zanzibar Town. The buds of the plant must be picked by hand and dried as shown. Photograph copyright © Camerapix, Kenya.

Historically, Zanzibar has been the gateway to Tanzania, a country that was at one time known as Tanganyika, for the lake on its western border, which includes the lowest point on the African continent. As it stretches to the northeast, Tanzania also encompasses the highest point on the continent, Mount Kilimanjaro. The eastern arm of the Great Rift Valley cuts through the central part of the country, which consists of a grassy savanna that gradually gives way to the coastal plains that lead to the Indian Ocean. Tanzania is thought by many anthropologists to be the original home of the human race.

In a country of such geological extremes, it is not much of a stretch to imagine that the block pattern on the plaited mat was meant to represent the highs and lows of the topography. Mountains, lakes, canyons, and plateaus—the angles of this geometric design could easily represent them all. The sisal grown and used by African women for baskets and mats is known as hedgerow sisal, as opposed to the sisal that has always been an important export crop for Tanzania and is grown and processed commercially.

Layout diagram

Making Tanzania Tiles

FABRIC REQUIREMENTS

Based on 42" to 44" (106 cm to 112 cm) selvage to selvage

Mulitcolor print for background and outer border	1¼ yd (115 cm)
Assortment of red prints for motifs and inside border	½ yd (45 cm)
Top border	⅛ yd (12 cm)
Outer border	½ yd (45 cm)
Backing	1⅝ yd (150 cm)
Binding	½ yd (45 cm)

Smart Piecing

As most quilters know, the center of an autograph block is like a nine-patch but the middle row is one piece, the better to write upon. The method we used results in tile blocks that look exactly like the traditional autograph block and is ever so easy to do. The finished block is 7″ × 7″ (17.5 cm × 17.5 cm).

1. For each block, cut as follows. Multiply by number of blocks needed (eight for "Tanzania Tiles"). Cut all pieces in one session, using a rotary cutter, ruler, and cutting mat.

   A squares: cut 4 of background fabric
       2½″ × 2½″ (6.5 cm × 6.5 cm)
   B squares: cut 10 of background fabric
       1½″ × 1½″ (4 cm × 4 cm)
   C squares: cut 8 of red print
       1½″ × 1½″ (4 cm × 4 cm)
   D rectangles: cut 4 of red print
       1½″ × 3½″ (4 cm × 9 cm)
   E rectangles: cut 1 of background fabric
       1½″ × 3½″ (4 cm × 9 cm)

2. You will piece block in rows, but first make four B/C/B units. Each consists of a red square flanked by two background squares. Then, sew each B/C/B unit to a D rectangle along one long side. Sew an A square to each end of two B/C/B/D units. These make top and bottom rows.

3. For center row, sew together two C/B/C units. Each consists of a background square in center flanked by two red squares. Sew one of these C/B/C units to each long side of an E rectangle. This is center square of quilt block. To complete center row, make two

Step 2

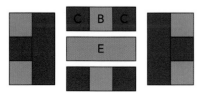

Step 3

Step 4

B/C/B/D units. Join each to a C/E/C unit on one side of center square, making sure rectangle D is against center square.

4. Complete quilt block by joining all three rows.

Setting the Blocks Together on the Diagonal

5. To complete quilt top, cut side and corner triangles. These pieces are a bit larger than needed. There will be enough excess to trim and straighten edges of quilt before joining borders to quilt. Cut as follows:

   For setting blocks, cut three squares
   7½″ × 7½″ (19 cm × 19 cm)
   For corner triangles, cut two squares
   7″ × 7″ (17.5 cm × 17.5 cm)
   Cut in half diagonally to make four half-square triangles
   For side triangles, cut two squares
   12″ × 12″ (30 cm × 30 cm)
   Cut twice diagonally to create eight quarter-square triangles

6. To sew diagonal sets, see "Kenya Four-Patch," page 68, steps 4 to 10, for cutting setting squares and outside triangles for a 7″ × 7″ (17.5 cm × 17.5 cm) square.

Borders

7. "Tanzania Tiles" is finished with three different borders, plus an extra strip at the top. Red inner border is randomly pieced from assorted red prints. To make it, cut 1½″ (4 cm) strips of red prints into random lengths and sew them together end-to-end until approximately 3½ yd (320 cm) long. Cut two lengths for side borders 40″ (100.5 cm), and sew in place. Cut 22¼″ (56 cm) lengths for top and bottom borders and sew in place.

8. For second (swirly print) border, cut two strips 2″ × 41½″ (5.5 cm × 105.5 cm); sew them to the red borders on the sides of the quilt. Cut two strips 2″ × 25″ (5 cm × 64 cm) and sew them to the red strips at top and bottom.

9. For extra strip at top of quilt, cut a strip 3½″ × 25″ (9 cm × 64 cm) and sew it in place to top swirly print border.

10. For the outside (striped) borders on sides, cut two strips 3″ × 48″ (8 cm × 121 cm), plus a little extra length for mitering corners. For top and bottom outside striped borders, cut two strips 3″ × 30¼″ (8 cm × 76 cm), plus a little extra for mitering corners. Sew strips in place without connecting them to one another at corners. See page 155 for directions on cutting extra length and mitering corners.

Quilting

11. To add batting and backing, see page 155. The quilting of "Tanzania Tiles" is done by machine with a varigated rayon thread in a free-motion design. See page 158 for instructions for applying a binding.

*He who marries beauty
marries trouble.*

Nigerian proverb

Fulani Stars

FULANI STARS

by Kaye England, 1999. 52" × 68" (130 cm × 173 cm).

Formed from a basic four-triangle block, three stars peep out of a background of mixed prints. The four-triangle block adds texture and interest to the stars' background, the stars in the border make an optical illusion of lozenges. "Fulani Stars" is a true scrap quilt. This is a good project to send you to your fabric stash to search out those pieces you've never quite gotten around to using—funky plaids, ugly prints, strange florals. They will all look great in this quilt—just keep in mind the type of overall color impression you want, whether earthy, airy, jungly, or whatever. It's generally a good idea to keep the color values in the light-to-medium range for all but the main stars, which have a deeper value.

The Fulani live in West Africa from Nigeria on the Atlantic coast, south into Cameroon, and north into Mali, Niger, and even into southwestern Chad. Although all Fulani speak a Nigritic language (one of the four major language types of Africa), they vary greatly in physical appearance and in the ways they make a living. Some are nomadic herders and farmers, moving about as the seasons change, generally back and forth across the Niger River, as far as three hundred miles on both sides. Of the Fulani that settle in one place, there is, in the northern river delta area, a group of weavers, artisans who have passed their techniques down through generations.

Because most Fulani are Islamic, they have a different design ethic from those groups who practice native religions and Christianity. Their religion forbids realistic images of animal or human forms, so they have become adept at creating

Fulani cavalrymen are dressed in quilted armor, as are their horses. The motif of the horse armor is the familiar four-triangle square, a basic motif in African design. Photograph copyright © Photo Researchers.

intricate and impressive abstract designs. Their faith instructs them to bring new converts to Allah, and the methods chosen for that vary according to individual factions. But sometimes this evangelicism becomes quite aggressive, and jihads, or holy wars, result. The Fulani depended on their horses in battle and made elaborate suits of quilted horse armor to protect them. (See also pages 44 and 123.)

The design for "Fulani Stars" was taken from a set of horse armor that used the basic four-triangle unit so common in American patchwork. As you study the quilt, you will find three stars—one red, one green, and one violet—in the design that quilters have come to know as "Ohio Star." You can choose how many stars you want; all you have to do is make sure all the points are the same color: as this quilt proves, the center square of the star doesn't even have to be the same color as the points.

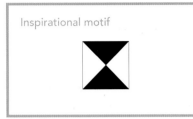

Inspirational motif

Layout diagram

Making Fulani Stars

FABRIC REQUIREMENTS

Based on 42″ to 44″ (106 cm to 112 cm) selvage to selvage

Scrap fabrics for pieced top and pieced border	3 to 4 yd (270 cm to 370 cm)
Inner and outer borders	½ yd (45 cm)
Backing	3 yd (270 cm)
Binding	½ yd (45 cm)

You will need the following units (all squares finish to 4″ [10 cm]):

46 four-triangle squares in a light/medium color scheme

12 four-triangle squares in a dark/light color scheme

56 unpieced squares in light and medium colors

3 unpieced squares in dark colors

Quick-Pieced Four-Triangle Squares

Step 1

Step 2

1. For medium/light stars, cut 23 light-colored print squares and 23 medium-colored print squares, each 5¼″ × 5¼″ (14 cm × 14 cm). For dark/light stars, cut six dark print squares and six light print squares of same size. Place a light square and a dark square right sides together, matching raw edges. Draw a line diagonally through the center from corner to corner. Stitch ¼″ (0.75 cm) on both sides of line.

2. Carefully cut along drawn line to make two triangle units. Open each unit and press flat; press seam allowances to darker side. Place triangle units together, with right sides facing and each light triangle against a dark triangle; snuggle the seams to one another, making sure seam allowances go in opposite directions. Draw a line diagonally from corner to corner. Stitch ¼″ (0.75 cm) on both sides of line.

Step 3

3. Cut along drawn line and press each half open. Repeat to assemble all remaining four-triangle units. You will have two complete four-triangle units, without ever having worked with a bias edge. If you cut out individual triangles and stitch four together, seams would all be on the bias and would likely stretch. This way, you have nice, flat four-triangle units.

Quilt Top Assembly

4. The solid squares and four-triangle squares are alternated in rows and columns, like a checkerboard. The four-triangle squares are placed in crosswise rows with darker bases at top and bottom; in lengthwise rows, darker bases go toward sides. These two kinds of rows alternate. Alternating direction of triangles not only adds a sense of movement, it causes stars to emerge. Place dark stars as desired. Just be sure to reserve light/dark four-triangle squares and three dark unpieced squares, because they form the visible stars. Only these areas of quilt must be planned; other fabrics can be completely random.

Borders

5. There are three borders on this quilt. For inside border, cut all strips 2½″ (6.5 cm) wide. Side strips, cut 52½″ (131.5 cm) long, go on first. Top and bottom strips are cut 40½″ (101.5 cm) long and go on next.

6. Middle border is pieced of 52 four-triangle squares, made with 26 light-colored and 26 medium-colored 5¼″ (14 cm) squares. To be sure border will fit, be as accurate as possible in cutting and sewing. If need be, adjust inside and outside borders to achieve a perfect fit. Sew 14 units together for each of the side borders and 10 units for top and bottom borders. Sew side borders in place, and then top and bottom ones.

7. Outside border is same fabric and width as inside border—2½″ (6.5 cm). Measure middle border after it is sewn to the quilt top to determine exact length required for outside borders. Outside border will be about 64½″ (163 cm) for sides and about 52½″ (132 cm) for top and bottom. Adjust length to fit measurement of quilt.

Quilting

8. To add batting and backing, see page 155. Body of this quilt was machine-stitched along all horizontal and vertical seams. Stitching was placed "in the ditch," using a "walking" presser foot. Upper thread is invisible thread, and lower thread is cotton. Stars have been highlighted by changing to a silver metallic thread. Quilting inside the stars meanders, but in a different pattern than in rest of the quilt. Each star was outlined in metallic ombré thread, couched in place with silver. See page 158 for instructions for applying a binding.

It is better to travel alone
than with a bad companion.
—Senegalese proverb

A View from the Edge

This familiar arrangement of equal-sized triangles was found on a beaded belt from Botswana. Interpreted in a sophisticated quilt design, the motif suggests a mountainous terrain. Study the finished quilt carefully and notice how the changes in values, from darks to lights and back again, suggest a horizon or perhaps a river. The strong diagonal line across the quilt implies some kind of barrier: another "view from the edge," if you will. Choose your favorite animal to enjoy this view.

The pieced background of this quilt is a design familiar to quilters, but its inspiration came from a motif on a Botswana beadwork belt. Botswana is inhabited by the Tswana, a subgroup of the Sotho-speaking Bantu people; *Botswana* actually means "land of the Tswanas." The country consists in large part of the Kalahari Basin, a land of great extremes. The temperature can range from 100 degrees in the summer to below freezing in the winter. The majority of the land is dry, not swampy, covered with scrub bushes and tree savannas.

The Kalahari is also the home of one of the few remaining aboriginal civilizations, that of the Bushmen. The Bushmen are known as cheerful, happy, and completely adapted to the rigorous conditions of the Kalahari—they are Stone Age people whose natural environment is slipping away from them.

Most of the Tswana people live in the eastern part of the country, in the Limpopo River watershed; it is the only land worth farming. Cash income has traditionally come from livestock, but more recently many Tswana have been employed in the diamond mines, which the government is developing as a commercial enterprise along with the mining of nickel, copper, and sulfur. Although modern houses of concrete block, lumber, and glass, complete with modern electrical appliances, are the norm today, a few of the traditional houses, made of dried mud with cone-shaped thatch roofs, can still be found in rural areas.

The tradition of beadwork among the Tswana is one they share with their close neighbors, the Ndebele. Tswana traditional dress, now almost completely replaced by Western-style clothing, included precisely patterned beaded belts and aprons. No doubt the geometry

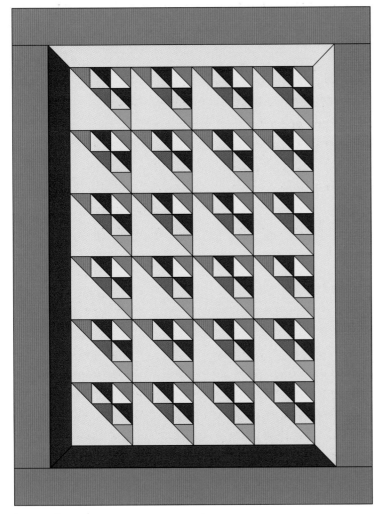

Layout diagram

of the triangular motif appealed to the Tswana craftswoman who used it on her beadwork belt, and that same characteristic has made it a familiar motif in quilting.

When this motif is used on its own as the solitary building block of a traditional American quilt design, it is known as "Sugar Loaf"; when a large, unpieced triangle is added to it so that a square is formed, the motif is known as "Birds in the Air." However, triangles pieced together in this manner can be found in any number of traditional quilt patterns: they can be used to form a half-block, as in this quilt, or they can form the corners for blocks that have a central motif. They are also wonderfully effective in various arrangements in the borders of a quilt.

Detail of "A View from the Edge." A star, cut with deliberately uneven points, is centered with a fierce mask taken from a print fabric. The mask is raw-edge appliquéd to the star, which is then applied in the same manner to the quilt top after all borders have been stitched in place. This close-up shows in detail three abstract designs for machine quilting.

Making A View from the Edge

FABRIC REQUIREMENTS

Based on 42" to 44" (106 cm to 112 cm) selvage to selvage

Light fabrics, assorted prints	1 yd (90 cm)
Medium-to-dark fabrics, assorted prints	1 yd (90 cm)
Inner border and star, dark pieces	⅛ yd (12 cm)
Inner border and star, light pieces	⅛ yd (12 cm)
Outer border	½ yd (45 cm)
For zebra (or monkey, crocodile, or parrot)	one section of fabric with motif
Backing	1½ yd (140 cm)
Binding	½ yd (45 cm)

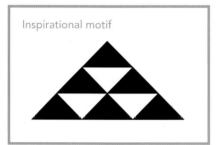

Inspirational motif

Piecing the Triangle Blocks

Half the basic block is a solid triangle, and the other half is made of pieced triangles. Within the pieced triangles are three squares, each made of two small triangles. Because the colors of the small triangles are meant to be randomly placed across the quilt, you should not make more than three or four squares in the same combination of fabrics. You can set up an assembly line by first cutting all the triangles you will need from pattern piece A. For 24 blocks, you will need 216 triangles. *Before you cut,* take into consideration that you must make two-thirds of your triangles in a dark color and one-third in a light color.

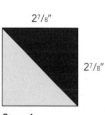

2⅞"

2⅞"

Step 1

1. Triangles are half-squares. Cut a 2⅞" (7.5 cm) square of fabric, then cut it in half on diagonal. From medium-to-dark fabrics, cut 144 triangles; from light fabrics, cut 72 triangles.

2. Each pieced half consists of three rows: row 1 has two squares and a triangle; row 2 has one square and one triangle; row 3 is one triangle. Begin by stitching together triangles to make three squares for each quilt block.

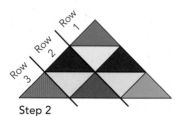

Row 1
Row 2
Row 3

Step 2

3. Now comes the fun part—placing of colors. Make pairs of your triangles, one light (or medium) and one dark. You can play with the pairing of colors to your heart's content. Make enough pairs to equal three times the number of blocks you need. Take pairs to your sewing machine and place them so that you can easily pick up one pair at a time and run it quickly under the needle of your sewing machine, making a ¼" (0.75 cm) seam. You do not

Step 3

Step 4

want to break your stitching—just make one long continuous chain of stitched-together triangles.

4. When you finish seaming all the triangles, take them to ironing board, clip them apart, and press seam toward dark triangle. Voilà! You will have a square, half light and half dark.

5. To complete pieced half of quilt block, stitch three squares and three triangles together in rows as in step 2. Another opportunity to have fun with color presents itself at this point; you can mix and match three squares and three triangles as you wish.

6. Study unpieced triangles in finished quilt to determine how many of each color you want. Quilt in the photograph shows five half-blocks of the light-colored "swimming snakes" fabric; three half-blocks *each* of medium-colored cheetah, grass, and sand-paintings fabrics; three half-blocks of bright medium-hued zebra print, and two half-blocks of a similar print; and four of a dark-colored gray, tan, and brown print. To cut your unpieced triangles, first cut a 6⅞" (17.5 cm) square, then cut it in half on the diagonal. Repeat until you have an assortment of 24 triangles in the fabrics you have chosen.

7. Pair up the pieced halves with the unpieced halves, again in the color combinations you like best. Stitch the two halves together, utilizing the continuous chain of stitching. Take the blocks to ironing board, clip apart, and press seam toward the large triangle.

Quilt Top Assembly

8. Sew blocks together into rows, placing solid triangles to run diagonally across quilt. Join rows together to make the field of quilt.

9. Sew the inner and outer borders to quilt top, mitering corners (see p. 155).

10. Carefully cut animal motif from background fabric. Place in position and pin or baste. Raw-edge appliqué the animal shape in place, stitching exactly on outline; edge will ravel and rough up, adding texture to piece.

11. Cut a star from any fabric you desire; ours has been embellished with an African mask from a printed fabric. The mask was raw-edge appliquéd to the star, and the star was then raw-edge appliquéd to the quilt top.

Quilting

12. To add batting and backing, see page 155. Because this is a busy quilt, it is best if an overall abstract pattern is chosen and machine stitched all over its surface. See page 158 for instructions for applying a binding.

Copying everyone else all the time,
the monkey one day cut his throat.

—Zulu proverb

Zulu Vista

◀ **ZULU VISTA**

by Kaye England, 1998. 52″ × 52″
(125 cm × 125 cm).

This quilt was inspired by the graceful
birds printed on an imported fabric. The
motif of the inside border is found in
many African cultures. In Adinkra
symbolism, it stands for the windmill,
which signifies the ability to withstand
life's adversities; to the Zulu, it represents
a married man. This quilt could easily
represent the scene that might greet you
as you travel the grassy plains of
Zululand. The habitat that supports the
Zulu's esteemed cows is also beneficial to
birds. Indeed, certain species of crane
follows the herds of cattle, catching the
insects that are stirred up as the cows
graze. The cranelike birds in this piece
(and in "The Antelope and the Goose")
are from an imported textile. You might
choose to make your own appliqué
design rather than taking one from a
printed fabric.

Six million Zulu now live in villages just north of Durban and
in the city itself, making them the largest ethnic group in
South Africa. The 10,000 square-mile reserve of Zululand
fronts the Indian Ocean on the eastern edge, is bounded by
mountains on the western border, and has semifertile plains with
many rivers and streams in between. Villages, each of which consists
of a very large extended family ruled by a chief, are typically shaped
like horseshoes, with a fence around the outside and a livestock pen in
the center. Most Zulu homes are constructed of straw and grass and
are dome-shaped, like a beehive.

As might be expected of a culture in which the men were fierce
warriors, the division of household labor is vastly unequal; women do

A very stylishly turned-out Zulu woman washes
clothes in a stream in South Africa. Her hairstyle
is accomplished by applying ocher to the strands
of hair, then stretching them over a lightweight
wooden frame. At night she sleeps with a special
headrest to protect her hairstyle. Photograph
copyright © Gerald Cubitt, South Africa.

far more work than do the men. In addition to cooking, cleaning, and caring for the children, the women repair the homes, collect water, carry and chop wood, and brew beer. They also make pots and weave baskets, employing many interesting decorative motifs in their work. Men clear the land of trees, build the homes, and tend the livestock.

Traditional dress for the women, which they still wear in the rural areas, consists of a long dress with a shawl. Married women often add black leather skirts to the ensemble and tint their hair red with clay; unmarried women wear their hair in a sort of ponytail. During courtship, young men and women adorn themselves with feathers, animal skins, love charms, and colorful beads. Red beads symbolize eyes weary from searching for a lost love; white represents love; green beads stand for resentment; and black is for unhappiness.

The Zulu have a deep belief in magic and often wear a profusion of lucky charms and amulets. They also believe in ancestor worship and think that departed spirits come back to this earth as snakes. When a snake enters a village, it is greeted with great ceremony, and often a sacrifice of a small goat is made to the snake. The Zulu celebrate birthdays, marriages, and deaths with elaborate group rituals and gatherings that feature dances and costumes.

Making Zulu Vista

Piecing a Landscape Background by Topstitching and Trimming

FABRIC REQUIREMENTS

Based on 42" to 44" (106 cm to 112 cm) selvage to selvage

Assortment of fabrics for background	1½ yd (140 cm)
Prints for birds and leaf forms	2 yd (180 cm)
Assortment of six fabrics for appliqué shapes, each	¼ yd (23 cm)
Assortment of six fabrics for pieced border, each	¼ yd (23 cm)
Three fabrics for outer border, each	¼ yd (23 cm)
Backing	3 yd (270 cm)
Binding	½ yd (45 cm)

Piecing the Landscape Background

1. Begin by estimating desired size of the background. You will work from top of piece toward the bottom. Choose "sky" fabric so that it is as wide as, but slightly longer than, you will need. Pick the second fabric according to effect you want—shadow, shading, or highlighting. Lay it over sky fabric, allowing a good overlap so that you can topstitch along top edge of the second fabric, which is cut to the desired shape—curved, pointed, or rolling. Place topstitching about ½" (1.25 cm) from cut edge, so that there will be a generous seam allowance to fringe and add texture. Turn piece over. Trim away extra length of sky fabric on back.

2. Add as many levels of color as you want, simply by topstitching each new level in place, trimming excess off the back of the preceding piece and fringing the seam allowance on the front.

TECHNIQUE

The landscape background is a perfect place to use the ¼-yard cuts you may have in your stash. You will need several pieces of different colors, keeping in mind that you will use different shades to create the illusion of a horizon with various features; ours includes a mountain. It is not necessary to think in terms of "blue for the sky and green for the grass." Think of rolling grasslands, fiery sunsets, pastel-tinted clouds. . . . The pieced border incorporates the fabrics used in the landscape background and the outer borders, as well as six to eight different red prints and as many brown prints. Notice that every block contains at least one red triangle (a nod to the Zulu respect for the color).

Vary shapes of the stitched edge. Notice that the mountain in this piece is made of cheetah fabric that has been carefully cut to reveal the individual animals; the "sky" is made of a flying bird print; and the highlighted section behind mountain is a "swimming snake" fabric. Foreground fabric is a grassy print, suggesting natural habitat of high-stepping birds.

3. Once broad strokes of landscape have been defined with your different bands of fabric, you can add in other shapes for interest. Leafy shapes grow up from lower edge, and vines are suggested by long slender shapes reaching in from left side. Primary shapes, birds and bushes, are appliquéd last so that they will be on top. Pieced border was sewn in place before final appliqué was completed.

Borders

4. Method of making the four-triangle square is explained in full in "Fulani Stars," page 97. Make 44 blocks, using 4¾″ (15 cm) squares. If you want your quilt to look like this one, be sure to include at least one red triangle per block.

5. Sew blocks into two lengths of 10 blocks each and two lengths of 12 blocks each. Alternate direction of light and dark triangles. Attach 10-block lengths to top and bottom edges of the landscape background, and 12-block lengths to the sides. (You can adjust borders to fit as needed by manipulating seams of blocks.)

6. For outer borders, piece together any two fabrics you like, cutting them first to a width of 5″ (13 cm). Measure length of borders and sew them in place (see page 155).

7. Press all border seams toward center of quilt. Examine quilt top for any additional areas that need pressing. Take care of problems before next step.

Quilting and Embellishing

8. To add batting and backing, see page 155. Texture and depth are incorporated into landscape by using lots of stipple quilting. Slopes of the landscape are emphasized by addition of rows of cowrie shells that are sewed securely onto fabric. Veins and striations of leaves are highlighted with beads sewed on top of lines. Sequins and beads are also scattered randomly across surface of the leaves, held in place with a dot of paint. The birds' eyes sparkle with jet beads. See page 158 for instructions for applying a binding.

TECHNIQUE

You can add lots of color and texture to a piece with a combination of paint and sequins—using a light touch, of course! Choose Tulip Paint™ in the color you want, and dab a small dot onto the quilt surface. Immediately place a flat sequin in the center of the dot, and use a straight pin to push the sequin down into the paint so it will seep over the edges. Allow the paint to dry 24 hours, and the sequin will be permanently secured.

Man is like palm wine: when young, sweet but without strength; in old age, strong but harsh.

—Congolese proverb

Congo Logs

The very word *Congo* evokes Africa, bringing to mind a dark, bottomless river that alternately glides, pools, and plunges through a dense jungle teeming with exotic wildlife. More than 2,600 miles in length, it is the seventh-longest river in the world. The people for whom this river and region were originally named are the Kongo, also known as the BaKongo. They inhabit large areas of Democratic Republic of Congo (Zaire), Congo, and Angola, all countries of West Africa that border one another.

The land of the Kongo is marked by rainforests in the upper, northern sections and savannas in the southern sections. Ancestors of the Kongo, the Bantu, occupied the region as early as the last millennium B.C. Perhaps in part because they have historically been farmers, today's six million or so Kongo are primarily vegetarians and enjoy a wide variety of fruits and vegetables, including maize, eggplant, tomatoes, beans, peanuts, bananas, and peppers. One of their specialties is palm wine, which is said to be sweet and intoxicating.

By the 1400s, the Kongo had built one of the most powerful kingdoms in the area. They established commerce with Portuguese traders who came to call at their Atlantic seaports. The Kongo chief controlled the east-west trade, from inland to the coast, and found dealing with Europeans profitable. Although the Kongo king converted to Christianity in 1491, his faith did not prevent his trafficking in the slave trade. For the next 300 years or so, the Kongo kings sold not only Africans from other kingdoms but also their own people into slavery. It has been said that the brisk slave trade almost completely depopulated some areas of the Congo.

Today, the Kongo are skilled craftspeople, noted for their metalwork and their wood and stone carving, especially of masks and small statues. Almost every Kongo home contains a fertility statue,

▶ Moraba-raba Logs

by Kathy Gwin, 1999. 42″ × 42″
(105 cm × 105 cm).

This chevron-type "Log Cabin" design
was taken from a motif painted on a
house in South Africa. The basic block is
even easier to construct than in "Congo
Logs," if that is possible. Study one, and
you will see how the 1-inch wide logs go
together. One diagonal row of machine
quilting anchors each block. The
remainder of the quilt is tied, and long
decorative ends are left on each knot for
embellishment.

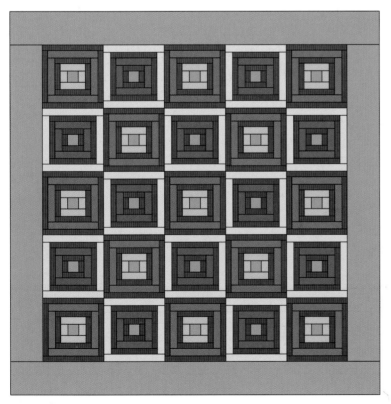

Layout diagram

represented by a mother and child,
carved either of soapstone or wood.
However, their fabrics made from palm
fibers have brought them worldwide
recognition. (See also page 33.)

The inpiration for both quilts
shown came from a rectangle-within-a-
rectangle design taken from a wooden
keg collected from the lower Congo
area, now in the Museé Royal de
l'Afrique Centrale Tervaren, in
Belgium. A similar motif, although it is
a square-within-a-square, was found
carved into a wooden piece from
Nigeria. It is in the Ipswich Museum in
Massachusetts.

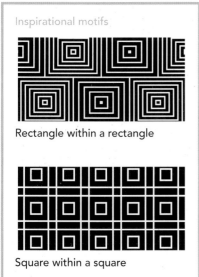

Rectangle within a rectangle

Square within a square

Making Congo Logs

Piecing a "Log Cabin" in the Courthouse Steps Style

FABRIC REQUIREMENTS

Based on 42" to 44" (106 cm to 112 cm) selvage to selvage

For center square of each block	½ yd (45 cm)
For first row of logs, each color	¾ yd (70 cm)
For second row of logs, each color	¾ yd (70 cm)
Black	1½ yd (140 cm)
Large-scale print for outer border	1 yd (90 cm)
Backing	3 yd (270 cm)
Binding	½ yd (45 cm)

Coloring Congo Logs

Each of the two colorations of the basic block in "Congo Logs" requires two different prints plus black. Choose two prints that contrast sharply with one another for each coloration. One block is done in warm colors and the other in cool colors. Also, the lightest band of color is on the outside in the cool color scheme and is in the middle in the warm colors. It doesn't matter where the lights and darks are placed within each color scheme, but they should be different. This design relies on high contrast for success. The exception is the center square, which has very subtle color, unlike an American "Log Cabin" quilt. Traditionally it was red, to represent the chimney of the cabin. Although it may no longer be red, the center square in American "Log Cabin" blocks is usually in high contrast to the other fabrics. However, because the center square of this African version represents the peak of a thatched roof, it should blend in, not call attention to itself. The center square is the same in each block.

Piecing the "Log Cabin" Block with Logs of Unequal Widths

This technique, a different way of piecing traditional "Log Cabin" square, uses strips of unequal widths. You may have discerned that black strips are slightly narrower than colored strips, and they frame colored areas of square. Each block finishes to 8½" (22 cm) square. Cut all strips for your blocks at one time, using a rotary cutter.

1. Block A is done in a warm color scheme; make a total of 13. Cut a 2″ (5.5 cm) center square for each block (13 squares). For first

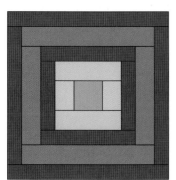

Step 1

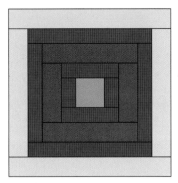

Step 2

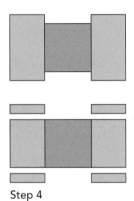

Step 4

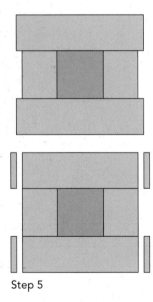

Step 5

round of "logs," cut 13 strips 1½" × 13½" (4 cm × 34 cm). For first round of black, cut 13 strips 1¼" × 21" (3.5 cm × 53 cm). For second round of "logs," cut 13 strips 1½" × 28" (4 cm × 70 cm). For outer round of black, cut 13 strips 1¼" × 36" (3.5 cm × 90 cm).

2. Block B is done in a cool color scheme; make 12. Cut a 2" (5.5 cm) center square for each block (12 squares). For first round of black, cut 12 strips 1¼" × 13" (3.5 cm × 33 cm). For first round of "logs," cut 12 strips 1½" × 20" (4 cm × 50 cm). For second round of black, cut 12 strips 1¼" × 27" (3.5 cm × 68 cm). For second round of "logs," cut 12 strips 1½" × 34" (4 cm × 85 cm).

3. Clip or pin strips for each block together or slip into a small plastic bag. Make one block at a time, being careful to alternate colored and black strips according to diagram. Always cut each strip just before sewing it in place, and always cut it with "room to spare," that is, a bit longer than needed. It is much easier and more accurate to lay strips in place and stitch without worrying about matching up ends. When you have sewed all the strips in one row together, they can be trimmed to an even width. This method of working results in a much squarer block.

4. To begin Block A, cut two strips of light-colored print fabric about 2½" (6.5 cm) long. Sew strips to center square, following "Courthouse Steps" style. First sew strips to opposite sides of center square; then trim seam allowances down to be even with the raw edge of the square. Press seam allowances away from center square.

5. Next, cut two strips of light-colored print fabric about 4¼" (11 cm) long and sew them across top and bottom of unit you made in previous step. Trim ends to even up square and press seam allowances toward solid strip.

6. To add the first round of black "logs," cut two black strips about 4½" (11.5 cm) long and sew them to either end of the square. Trim ends of strip flush with block. Press seam allowances toward black strip. Next, cut two black strips about 6" (15 cm) long. Sew them to the top and bottom of the square. Trim the ends. Press seam allowance toward black strip. Continue sewing strips and trimming and pressing until block is completed, making two more rounds of strips. Repeat for each block.

7. Make all Block Bs similarly, but reverse colored and black strips.

Quilt Top Assembly

8. Complete 25 blocks. Sew them together into five rows of five blocks, alternating blocks A and B. Note that three rows contain three of Block A and two of Block B, and two rows contain two of Block A and three of Block B. Sew rows so that blocks continue to alternate.

Border

9. Cut two border strips, each 43″ × 5″ (111.5 cm × 12.5 cm). Sew to sides of the quilt.
10. Cut two border strips, each 52″ × 5″ (113.5 cm × 12.5 cm). Sew to top and bottom.

Quilting and Embellishing

11. To add batting and backing, see page 155. As with most "Log Cabin" quilts, this one seems perfectly adapted for outline quilting of each log, ¼″ (0.75 cm) on each side of all seams. We also outline-quilted motifs in oversize print of border fabric, with one row of stitching to define each shape. See page 158 for instructions for applying a binding.

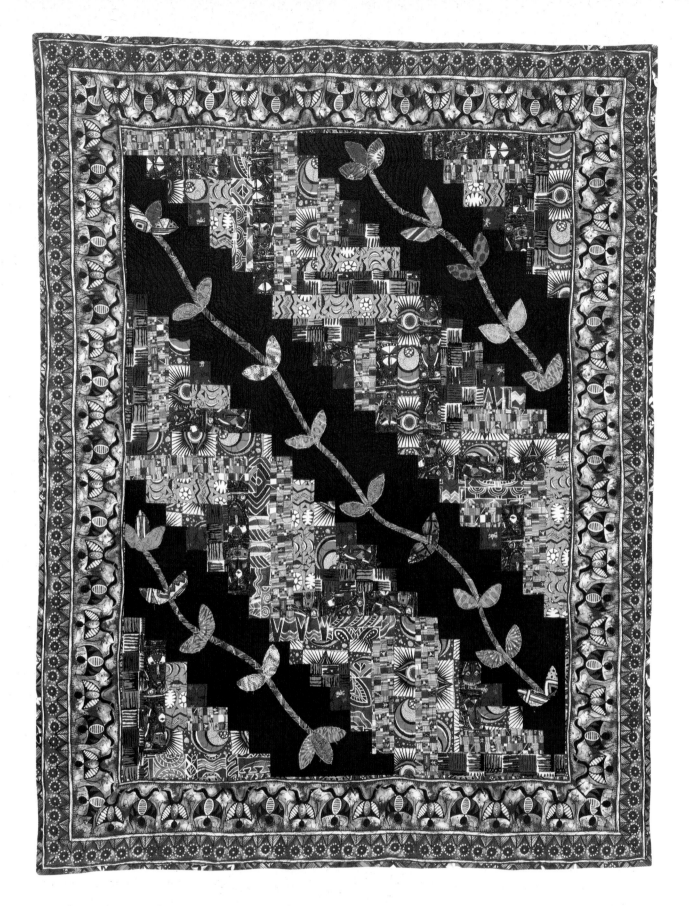

It is only the water that is spilt; the calabash is not broken.
—Mauritanian proverb

Kalahari Calabash

◀ KALAHARI CALABASH
by Kaye England and Laurie Keller,
1998. 56″ × 72″ (142 cm ×
183 cm).

The "straight furrows" of this traditional
"Log Cabin" setting provide the perfect
place for a gourd vine to grow. This
piece proves that African-themed quilts
can harmonize beautifully with a variety
of decorating styles and settings, from
country to contemporary, from study to
bedroom to living room—it would be
difficult to imagine an environment this
quilt would not complement. The print
used to finish the quilt is a border design
that appears to be two fabrics. It is cut so
that, at the very inside, next to the field
of the quilt, a narrow line of color
shows, giving the impression of piping.

A bottle fashioned from a calabash by
the Thonga of Mozambique. A hole
was pierced in the top, and the gourd
was decorated with incisions, dye, and
white beads. Photographs document
the use of such containers as milk
bottles by children of the Dinka,
pastoral nomads of the lower Nile
valleys. Photograph copyright © UCLA
Fowler Museum of Cultural History/
Photograph by Denis J. Nervig.

Africa is rich in plant life, and indigenous peoples all across the continent, through centuries of experimentation, have learned how to make the most of it. One of the most useful and ancient of plants is the calabash, or gourd. African farmers learned the gourd's usefulness early on and have shaped calabashes into spoons, ladles, masks, musical instruments, and even articles of clothing.

If the outer surface of the calabash is thick enough, it can be carved, as the Yoruba discovered, but most often the design is incised with a hot metal blade. In Cameroon, gourds were covered with beadwork in intricate and colorful patterns, and often sealed with a beadwork stopper shaped like an animal (see photograph on page 23). Other cultures have used basketry or leatherwork to decorate calabashes and make them more useful. Leather straps may be attached for carrying, and the Mangbetu women of Zaire weave grasses into lids.

The Fon tribe of Dahomey believes that the universe is made of

two calabash halves, one forming the dome of the sky and the other the bowl of sea and land. This belief about calabashes and the skill that goes into their decoration helps explain why so many families cherish them and pass them down from generation to generation. Cracked calabashes are often repaired with grasses or other fibrous materials, with the results often resembling fine embroidery.

Making Kalahari Calabash *Keeping a "Log Cabin" Square; Applying a Vine*

FABRIC REQUIREMENTS

Based on 42" to 44" (106 cm to 112 cm) selvage to selvage

Light logs, assortment of five prints, including

rust-red for center squares	1 yd (90 cm)
Black for dark logs	3 yd (270 cm)
Brown print for stem of vines	¾ yd (70 cm)
Leaves	Scraps
Backing	4 yd (360 cm)
Binding	½ yd (45 cm)
Border print	2¼ yd (205 cm)

Layout diagram

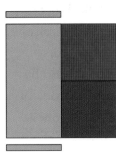

Step 3

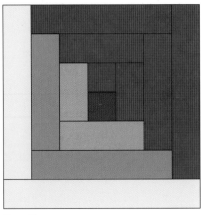

Step 5

Making the "Log Cabin" Block

Make 12 blocks. Half of each is made from various prints, other half is from solid black. Each block finishes out to 14" (35 cm) square.

1. Cut each print and black fabric into 2½" (6.5 cm) strips. Cut 12 center squares of rust-red print, measuring 2½" × 2½" (6.5 cm × 6.5 cm). Cut 12 black center squares same size.

2. Begin each block by sewing red and black center squares together. Press seam toward black.

3. Add a black "log" to one side of center squares and then a print "log" across the top of first black log and center square. There is no need to cut logs to specific lengths ahead of time. Simply cut each log from your fabric strip as you add it to the block, making it a bit longer than needed. You can always trim after you've sewn it in place. Stitching and trimming in this manner practically guarantees a good square block.

4. Choose a different print for the second "log" and add it to one side of the unit so that it goes across the top of first print "log"; sew a black log to other side of the unit. Press seam allowances to last sewn strip each time.

5. Keep working outward from center, adding print "logs" to print side and black "logs" to the black side until you've made three complete rounds.

Setting

6. Follow layout diagram to set blocks together into four rows of three blocks, placing light and dark sides to form "straight furrows" of color.

Applying a Vine

7. Cut stem of vine on bias ½" (1.25 cm) wide. Place vine strips on black section of quilt, forming curves. Pin loosely in place and then zigzag stitch along center line of vine. Allow edges to curl up; it adds texture to the piece. Use pattern A on page 169 to cut pairs of leaves from any fabrics desired. Notice that each vine ends with three leaves.

Borders

8. Cut top and bottom border strips equal to width of quilt top, plus twice width of stripe in border print, plus ½" (1.5 cm) for seam allowance. Our border is 7½" (18.75 cm) wide, so we cut strips 15½" (39 cm) longer than width of quilt.

9. Measure length of the quilt top and use the same formula to cut side borders.

10. Sew each border in place on all four sides of the quilt, leaving extra length loose; do not sew the borders to each other.

11. Miter corners, as explained on page 155.

Quilting

12. To add batting and backing, see page 155. Machine quilt ¼" (0.6 cm) on either side of each seamline and along curves of calabash vine. Zigzag stitching is used on the outer edges of leaf shapes, and centers of some are "veined" with machine feather stitching. See page 158 for instructions on binding quilt.

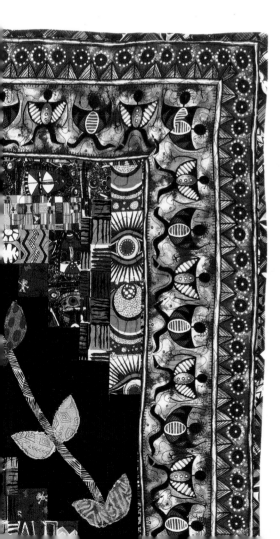

The rainbow is the sky serpent that transmits heavenly energy to the earth.
—African proverb

Sky Serpents

The rainbow is a sacred symbol in many cultures, especially by the BaKongo of the Democratic Republic of Congo (Zaire). The BaKongo of ancient times feared the raging thunderstorms that came in from the Atlantic and saw the rainbow as a strong giant arching his body over their village to protect it.

Except in the rainforests, the coming of rain in Africa is an event eagerly anticipated, prayed for, and gratefully received. For people who traditionally live in harmony with earth's rhythms, the end of the dry season is a time of thanksgiving and renewal. For example, two favorite colors across Africa are dark blue and black,

This colorful set of horse armor from the Sudan is quilted of many layers to protect the horse from arrows and other weapons of battle. It dates from about 1899 and incorporates the familiar "Flying Geese" patchwork pattern in red, gold, black, and purple. It inspired the accompanying quilt. Collection of The British Museum, London.

reputedly chosen because they are the colors of rain clouds—the darker the better, because dark clouds hold the most rain. In some cultures, rain clouds were actually regarded as an expression of divine power or as gods themselves. The proverb "Clouds are better than lightning" recalls lightning preceding rain.

The animist religions of much of Africa honor rain gods and goddesses. One of the most colorful resides in the Drakensburg (Dragon) Mountains of South Africa and is known as Mujaji the Rain Goddess or the Transformer of the Clouds. She can send turbulent rainstorms to wash away the houses of her enemies or cause a gentle rain to fall on the crops of those she loves. Her daughters ruled as Rain Queens. Many legends tell about their wisdom and cunning as they resisted the Boers and the British in the late nineteenth century.

There is great belief in rainmakers across the continent. When the Christian and Islamic prayers and hymns for rain ring out, many magicians and medicine men enact rituals to force the sky to drop rain through the magical power of the rainmaker. Rain dances, rain songs, and sacred rain stones, obtained from the heart of an ancestral king, are used, as are magical accessories such as an antelope horn stuffed with "medicines," including seashells and seaweed. A tribe of Kenya, the Nandi, push a white sheep into the river; when the sheep clambers back on the bank and shakes himself dry, the flying drops will bring rain.

The serpent or snake is regarded completely differently in African native religions than in the Bible, where it is always a symbol of evil. In Africa, snakes may be messengers from the spirit world or from ancestors. They may even be regarded as spirits or gods themselves. The Zulu believe a powerful king may be reincarnated as a mamba, a long, slender, tree-dwelling poisonous snake, and they believe that snakes contain the spirits of dead ancestors and would not think of killing one that enters a village. When the Zimba of Mozambique pray for rain, they carry the women, who are believed to be possessed of snake spirits at the time, into the forest to pray. The snake spirits love to watch the women dance and may be persuaded to answer perplexing health questions as messengers from the ancestors or the gods.

The name of this quilt, "Sky Serpents," comes from the long rows of triangular motifs that run the length of the quilt. The motifs are taken from a set of horse armor made by the Fulani people of the southern Sahara and Niger River delta. (See also page 95.)

Making Sky Serpents

FABRIC REQUIREMENTS

Based on 42" to 44" (106 cm to 112 cm) selvage to selvage

Color 1 for geese, assorted prints	1¼ yd (115 cm)
Color 2 for geese, assorted prints	1½ yd (140 cm)
Background for geese	2⅞ yd (260 cm)
Outer border and one row of geese	1½ yd (140 cm)
Inner border	⅓ yd (30 cm)
Backing	4¼ yd (385 cm)
Binding	½ yd (45 cm)

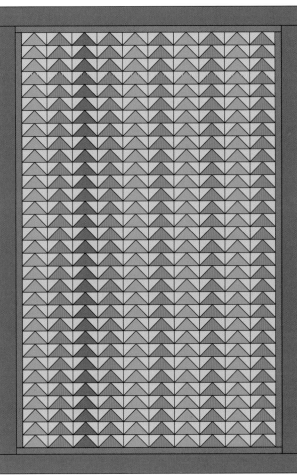

Layout diagram

Making Three-Dimensional Flying Geese

Part of the fun of making this quilt is assembling the fabrics; in the one shown, there are 10 different teals and 10 different greens. So, if you are passionate about a particular color or two, here's an opportunity to indulge yourself! The same background color is used throughout the quilt. A surprise is that one row of geese is pieced from the same fabric as the outer border and placed off-center in the quilt top. Three-dimensional piecing, used to make the geese, is difficult to explain on paper but amazingly easy to do. Try making one, and you'll see how much simpler it is to make a three-dimensional flying goose than a traditional stitched one. This outer border was chosen because of its "rainbow" design, an appropriate accompaniment to "flying geese"!

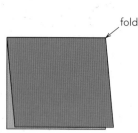

fold

Step 2

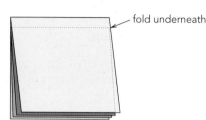

fold underneath

Step 3

Step 4

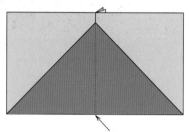

seam under goose

Step 5

The narrow 19 (2.5 cm) inner border is made of hot pink, chosen for its shock value, like the strongest ray of a rainbow.

There are 32 geese in each row. Make four rows of color 1, five rows of color 2, and one row with border fabric. Each finished unit is 2″ × 4″ (5 cm × 10 cm).

1. For each flying geese unit, cut one 2½″ × 4½″ (6.5 cm × 11.5 cm) rectangle (triangular "goose" when finished) and two 2½″ (6.5 cm) squares (background).

2. Fold the rectangle in half crosswise, wrong sides together.

3. Sandwich folded rectangle between two squares, right sides together. Align cut edges. Folded edge of rectangle will be ¼″ (0.75 cm) inward from one edge of squares.

4. Stitch a seam ¼″ (0.75 cm) from right or left edge of unit. Make sure not to sew along folded or bottom edge of rectangle. Clip tiny section of fold so that seam allowances lie open and flat. Press seam open.

5. Turn unit to right side, open it up, and pull the corners of "goose" to outside. Press flat.

TECHNIQUE

Alternative Method If you prefer, you can make flat flying geese, rather than three-dimensional ones. An easy way is the "connector" method of piecing. Cut a rectangle 2½″ × 4½″ (6.5 cm × 11.5 cm) and two 2½″ (6.5 cm) squares. Follow directions given with "Rainforest Stars," page 142.

Quilt Top Assembly

6. Make ten rows of 32 units each: five rows of teal fabrics, four rows of green fabrics, and one row of border print. When you begin to sew flying geese units together, you will realize why you need that ¼″ (0.75 cm) above fold—it gives a seam allowance that keeps the tip of each "goose" from being chopped off when they are sewn together.

7. Sew the rows together, alternating teal and green and placing row made with border fabric where a green row would be. You might want to turn one row in the opposite direction—have the geese fly south, just to add a little humor.

Borders

8. Measure your quilt top for correct length of borders (see page 155). Inside (hot pink) border is cut 1½″ (4 cm) wide. Outside (rainbow) border is cut 4″ (10.5 cm) wide. Corners are not mitered.

Quilting

9. To add batting and backing, see page 155. Because the three-dimensional flying geese are so interesting, the quilting is secondary. Use simple outline quilting to emphasize the three-dimensional geese. See page 158 for instructions on binding the quilt.

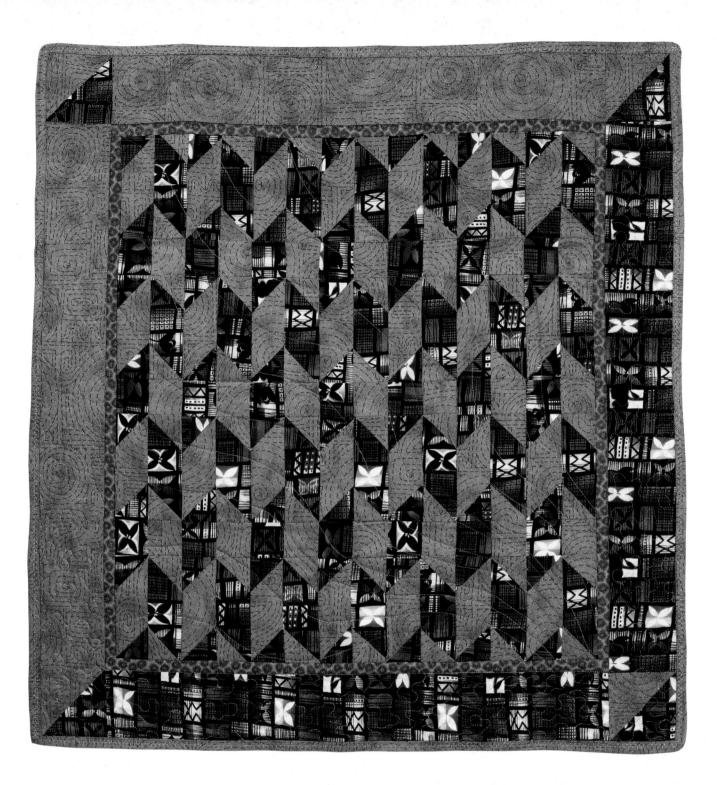

A pretty basket does not prevent worries.

—Zairian proverb

Bushongo Magic

◀ BUSHONGO MAGIC

◀ BUSHONGO MAGIC
by Kaye England, 1999. 29″ × 31″
(74 cm × 75 cm).

The Bushongo motif was going to be a
border for a quilt, but when the strips
were laid out side by side, the design for
an entire quilt magically appeared. This
quilt is made from two fabrics, a dark
print and a monotone print, which
appears as a medium-toned ochre.

W hether stationary or nomadic, all African families
traditionally made their homes and furnishings from
whatever natural materials were available. Essential to
most cultures were mats, made of plant materials such as palm leaves,
banana leaves, or grass. Mats, made in many sizes, could be woven,
plaited, or sewn. There are even accounts of overlapping raffia mats
being used as roof tiles on houses deep in the equatorial jungle.

A French traveler who visited a king's camp in Senegal, on the
upper West African coast, remarked in his *Voyage to Timbuktu*, written
during the years 1825-1830:

> *The king's bed is made
> . . . as a sort of platform
> covered with reed mats, held by
> crossboards and stakes, about
> one foot off the ground. A reed
> mat on the floor fills the rest of
> the space under the tent and
> provides a bed for the king's
> suite. The common people sleep
> on the floor on reed mats, which
> are occasionally covered with
> some straw.[1]*

A Betsileo woman weaves a hat out of
straw. Photograph copyright © Carl
D. Walsh/Aurora.

A sewn mat from the Democratic Republic of Congo featured alternating parallelograms.

Part of the reason that mats are used so widely is that they provide a cool surface, whether used as beds, covers, seats, rugs, or wall hangings. But even these everyday, utilitarian items are beautifully decorated, in patterns ranging from geometrics to stylized animals.

The weaving of plant materials into household items such as mats is a concept easily transferable to our modern culture. However, plant materials also provided interesting articles of personal adornment, as evidenced by the Mangbetu women of Zaire and their *cache-fesses* (buttock shields). Fan-shaped ovals 10″ to 12″ (15 cm to 30 cm) across, they were decorated with intricate designs, which were apparently a point of great pride and the source of some competition among the women. The Mangbetu women also used their skills at weaving plant materials to make fabulous baskets. Some were actually watertight and used to hold beer; other baskets held foodstuffs or cosmetics.

The name Bushongo figures prominently in the history of the Congo. Nyimi Bushongo was a successor to the great king Shamba Bolongongo, who reigned in the early seventeenth century, and is generally credited with being the father of his kingdom. Nyimi Bushongo's name means "elipse of the sun," for an event that occurred on his birthdate March 30, 1680. Bushongo's descendants continued to rule their portion of the Democratic Republic of Congo until they were defeated by the Belgians in 1904.

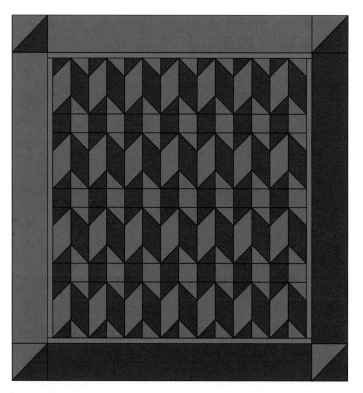

Layout diagram

Making Bushongo Magic

Quick Piecing with
Pairs of Connectors

FABRIC REQUIREMENTS

Based on 42" to 44" (106 cm to 112 cm) selvage to selvage

Dark print	¾ yd (70 cm)
Monotone print	¾ yd (70 cm)
Narrow inner border	⅛ yd (12 cm)
Backing	1 yd (90 cm)
Binding	⅓ yd (30 cm)

Making Connector Pairs

Connectors simplify the piecing of a difficult-looking pattern by reducing the need to work with tiny pieces and bias edges that might stretch and distort a seam. As building blocks of the quilt, they sometimes take an unexpected shape, but they make the work go much faster. Using connectors was explained in "Yoruba Dash," page 79. They were also used in "Adinkra Symbols," page 73. The difference here is that the basic unit in this quilt is a chevron made up of a pair of connectors. Notice that in each vertical row, the colors are the reverse of those in the preceding row, forming chevrons that are half light and half dark. The chevrons march across the quilt in four rows of seven chevrons each. The horizontal rows are set together with a spacer row of squares in between. However, because you attach the spacer squares to the basic unit, there is no need to go to the extra step of making a spacer strip—the entire quilt goes together as you put the basic units together. (The spacer squares are also part of an additional row of chevrons, as you may have noticed.) Although the quilt looks as though it is constructed with vertical rows of parallelograms, it's actually much easier to assemble in larger units.

1. Each basic chevron unit is made up of two rectangles measuring 2" × 5" (5.25 cm × 12.75 cm), one light and one dark, with two 2" (5.25 cm) square connectors per rectangle. Cut 28 rectangles and 56 squares of light fabric. Cut same numbers of dark fabric. In addition, cut 21 squares of each fabric for spacers.

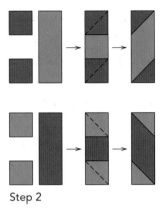

Step 2

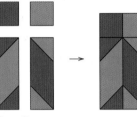

Step 3

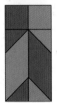

Step 4

2. To stitch connectors, lay a square at end of a rectangle, right sides together. Stitch diagonally from corner to corner of square. Trim away inside of square. Press triangle up, making raw edges even. Attach another connector to opposite end of rectangle, making sure diagonal seams are parallel. Make all dark-on-light units, then all light-on-dark units, reversing direction of triangles.

3. Sew a spacer square to end of each unit as shown and then sew a pair of units together so a light/dark chevron is formed. Make 21 chevron units. The final row of seven chevrons will not require spacer blocks.

Quilt Top Assembly

4. Sew three chevron/spacer units into a vertical row. Top it off with a plain chevron unit without a spacer. Make a total of seven rows. Sew rows together side by side, taking care to keep chevrons pointing in same direction in all rows. A secondary chevron pattern emerges as rows are joined.

Borders and Corner Squares

5. Cut strips for bright blue inside border 1″ × 23″ (2.5 cm × 59 cm) for sides, 1″ × 21½″ (2.5 cm × 55 cm) for top and bottom. Sew the strips in place, first on sides of quilt, then on top and bottom.

6. To make corner blocks, cut two 4⅞″ (12.5 cm) squares from each fabric. Cut each square in half diagonally through center. Group triangles in pairs, one of each color. Place right sides together and join along diagonal edge. Press seam allowances open.

Step 6

7. Cut two outside border strips 4½″ × 23½″ (11.5 cm × 60 cm) for the sides, and two for the top and bottom that measure 4½″ × 21½″ (11.5 cm × 55 cm). Sew a border strip to the top and bottom edges of quilt. Attach a corner square to each end of side border strips, watching placement of colors of triangles. Sew these border/corner block units to the sides of quilt. (Notice that the corner blocks give you "cheater miters" in two corners.)

Quilting

8. To add batting and backing, see page 155. Because tone-on-tone ocher print is done in circular patterns, a gently curving overall design was used to quilt body of this piece. Curves also provide a nice contrast to straight lines and angles of parallelograms. See page 158 for instructions on binding the quilt.

It is the duty of children to wait on elders,
not elders on children.

—Kenyan proverb

GoGo and the Veil of Rashaida

◀ **GOGO AND THE VEIL OF RASHAIDA**

by Kaye England, 1999. 43½″ × 43½″ (115 cm × 115 cm).

"This quilt was really a vision," says Kaye England about the inspiration that came to her after she learned the Ndebele word for grandmother and saw an Ndebele house painted with a "Grandmother's Choice" star. "I designed it on New Year's Eve and pieced it on January 1, 1999. It just seemed to speak to me and it continues to. I just love it." Kaye was further enchanted by the geometric motifs embroidered on an Islamic woman's veil and adapted them for a border.

In Ndebele society, the grandmother, or *GoGo*, is treated with great reverence and respect, and, in fact, rules the home. With no knowlege of quilt patterns or their names, a Ndebele artist chose to paint her house with a traditional star design known to quilters as a variation of "Grandmother's Choice." This happy coincidence suggests that the block of this quilt designed and named itself!

The "veil of Rashaida" refers to the *burga*, a heavy black cloth veil that is worn by the Rashaida, a group of nomadic orthodox Muslims who live in the Horn of Africa, in the Nubian Desert. They crossed the Red Sea from Saudi Arabia some 150 years ago, and believe that women must always be veiled as a gesture of modesty, although no objection is raised

Counter to most traditions, it is the Tuareg men who veil themselves, rather than the women. The women cover their hair with a headscarf, but the veiling of the men is more significant. Since the face is hidden except for the eyes, the identity of a man is known by the way he drapes his veil. Because of perspiration caused by the hot climate, the dye in the *tagelmust* often colors the faces and heads of the Tuareg. They have been called the "Blue Men of the Desert." Photograph copyright © Georg Gerster/National Geographic Image Collection.

to the elaborate decoration of the veil with embroidery and silver and gold jewelry, even coins.

In most Islamic cultures, women wear the veils. An exception is found with the Tuareg, one of the indigenous people of North Africa. Nomadic, tough, and mysterious, the Tuareg have long led camel caravans across the Sahara, traveling where others have been unable to find a path. The men traditionally wear veils, elaborately draped around the head to conceal everything but the eyes. It is thought that the purpose of the veil—especially if it is indigo-dyed—is to ward off the evil eye. Many cultures believe blue wards off evil spirits.

A Tuareg man must never remove his veil, even to sleep, once he receives it in late adolescence, although it can be dropped to the level of the chin among family and close friends while in camp. Tuareg men eat in public by slipping their food underneath their veils. A man is recognized by the distinctive manner of draping his veil and turban, or *tagelmust;* each develops his own style.

The influences that shaped this quilt come from the geographical extremes of the continent—North Africa, in the Sahara, and South Africa, outside the Kalahari. Even though the Ndebele and the Islamic Tuareg and Rashaida are a continent apart, their environments are similar. The primary difference is that the Ndebele are not nomadic, neither are they primarily Islamic, although their choice of geometric motifs for their art might indicate otherwise.

Layout diagram

Making GoGo and the Veil of Rashaida

FABRIC REQUIREMENTS

Based on 42" to 44" (106 cm to 112 cm) selvage to selvage

Solid black	½ yd (45 cm)
Purple print on dark background (includes binding)	1 yd (90 cm)
Purple print on light background	1 yd (90 cm)
Backing	1½ yd (140 cm)

Making Magic Stars

The magic in these stars is that you don't have to cut any triangles, so you don't have to worry about any stretchy bias edges. The star points are made by sewing squares onto one end of a rectangle and folding them back on themselves, a technique very similar to the connectors devised by Mary Ellen Hopkins. When four of these units are sewn to a center square, there's your star. The corners are filled in with squares. Your finished block measures 8½" (22.75 cm) square.

1. All stars are made from the dark background print. Cut nine 3" (7.75 cm) squares, one for the center and eight for the points. For the background of star, cut four rectangles 3" × 3½" (7.75 cm × 9 cm) and four 3½" (9 cm) squares of light background print.

2. Sort squares for points into pairs; one is a right side and one is a left side. Turn squares wrong side up. Locate center of one side on each. Use a ruler to mark an accurate point ⅛" (0.4 cm) left of center on right side point, and ⅛" (0.4 cm) right of center on left side of point. Now, on opposite side of each square, mark a point ⅛" (0.4 cm) in from outside corner; join this point to first one with a pencil line. This marks sewing line.

3. Choose one end of the light-colored rectangle and lay one square on it, right sides together, aligning cut edges. Stitch exactly on drawn line. Fold the square to right side on seamline. Press. Trim edges of square even with rectangle.

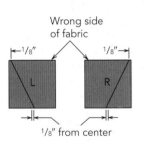

Wrong side of fabric

L   R

⅛"   ⅛"

⅛" from center

Step 2

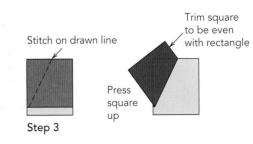

Stitch on drawn line

Trim square to be even with rectangle

Press square up

Step 3

Repeat for second side

Step 4

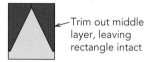

Trim out middle layer, leaving rectangle intact

Step 5

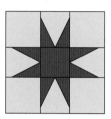

Step 6

4. Repeat Step 3 for other side, overlapping first point with second.

5. Trim away middle layer, leaving base rectangle intact. Press. Make four units.

6. Set star blocks together in three rows. Top row consists of a corner background square, a point unit, and another corner background square. Center row has two point units and star center square (be sure points go in right direction). Third row is same as top, but points are reversed. After rows are made, sew them together, press, and there's your star block. Make eight blocks.

Sashing and Corner Blocks

7. Sashing unit is made from three long strips, each cut from selvage to selvage. Cut a 2″ (5.25 cm) strip from light background fabric. Cut two black strips, each 1″ (2.5 cm) wide. Sew strips together lengthwise, with wider strip in center. Press seams to one side. Cut as many 9″ (24.25 cm) sashing units as possible from the strip. Piece additional strips to make 24 sashing units.

8. Cut 16 3″ × 3″ (7.25 cm × 7.25 cm) corner blocks from dark background print.

Quilt Top Assembly

9. Sew blocks into three rows, each containing three blocks with a sashing unit between each block in a row. Press seam allowances toward sashing. Use remaining sashing and corner blocks to make four sashing rows by alternating four corner blocks with

three sashing units in each row. Press seams toward corner blocks. Sew rows together.

Border

Step 10

Step 11

Step 12

Step 13

10. For A units, cut a 4½" (12.5 cm) square of each of both prints; place them right sides together. Draw a line diagonally through center of square, then sew a seam ¼" (0.75 cm) on each side of line. Cut apart on drawn line. Press seams open. Place pieces together again, right sides together so that opposite colors face each other. Again, draw a diagonal center line in unseamed direction, and stitch on either side of drawn line. Cut apart. Two units are formed. Trim units to a precise 3½" (9 cm) square.

11. For B units, cut a base rectangle of light background print 3" × 3½" (7.75 cm × 9 cm). Cut two 3" (7.75 cm) squares and join them following the connector method (see "Magic Stars," pages 137–138).

12. For C units, cut three 1" (2.75 cm) strips of black fabric from selvage to selvage. Cut two 1½" (4 cm) strips from light background fabric. Sew strips together lengthwise, beginning with a black strip and alternating with light. Press seams toward darker fabric. Square up one end and cut 3½" (9 cm) segment from long strip set. Repeat if you need more segments.

13. For D units, cut two 1¼" (3 cm) strips of black fabric from selvage to selvage. Cut two 1¼" (3 cm) from light background fabric. Sew strips together lengthwise, beginning with a black strip and alternating with light. Press seams toward darker fabric. Square up one end and cut segments from strip as long as needed. These units work especially well at ends of borders, because they can be trimmed to make border fit quilt.

Quilting

14. To add batting and backing, see page 155. Choose a quilting design from pages 170-175 if you wish or try free-motion quilting with a varigated metallic thread. Little embellishment is needed if the fabrics have strong patterns, as in this combination, especially with black accents. See page 158 for instructions on binding quilt.

When the bee comes to your house, let her have beer;
you might want to visit the bee's house someday.
—Congolese proverb

Rainforest Stars

Along the equator in Africa lies the rain belt. Every day, at the same time, a thunderstorm bursts out of the heavens and drenches the earth. The heavy rainfall and little temperature variation (less than one degree between the hottest and coldest days of the year) has provided an ideal environment for animals and plants, which grow in abundance in the rainforest. The vegetation can be so thick and the atmosphere so steamy that it is sometimes called the "green hell." It is the jungle.

The Bambuti Pygmies, of just such a steaming jungle, are probably one of the world's oldest peoples. Completely adapted to life in this demanding environment, they say: "A hungry pygmy is a lazy pygmy," because a wealth of game and other foodstuffs are easily available. According to the season, pygmy women spend much of their day gathering edible bulbs, berries, mushrooms, and other vegetation. The men deserve their reputation as skilled hunters, and, indeed, their skill with blowguns and poisoned darts is legendary. Long reluctant to leave their rainforest hideaway, the pygmies have gradually succumbed somewhat to the lures of civilization in that they interact with the tourists around the Ituri forest of the

Very little is known of the pygmies who inhabit the Congo rainforests. This pygmy mother and her child wear face paint to ward off danger. Like his mother and father, the child is likely to reach a height of no more than 4½ feet (140 cm). Photograph copyright © G. Philippart de Foy/Photo Researchers.

Layout diagram

Democratic Republic of Congo, selling them bows, arrows, and other items.

Until fairly recently, only the pygmies knew the okapi, found only in the Ituri forest, a habitat the two share. Although it is "tall and robust as a horse, but graceful as a doe," the best description of it is that it is a short-necked giraffe. It is an extremely wild and shy beast, and very little is known of it. Who knows what other secrets the rainforest holds?

Making Rainforest Stars   *Strippy Setting*

FABRIC REQUIREMENTS

Based on 42″ to 44″ (106 cm to 112 cm) selvage to selvage

Red print for outside borders, setting triangles, center of star blocks	1½ yd (140 cm)
Print for center strip and inside borders	1½ yd (140 cm)
Yellow fabric for background of stars	½ yd (45 cm)
Blue fabric connectors for star points	⅓ yd (30 cm)
Backing	2½ yd (230 cm)
Binding	½ yd (45 cm)

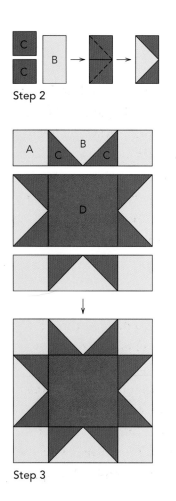

Step 2

Step 3

Piecing the Stars

1. Each star block finishes to 8″ (20 cm) square. Piecing is done with connectors; you actually cut no triangles! For each of 10 blocks cut the following:

   Yellow fabric, four squares A
   2½″ (7.5 cm)
   Yellow fabric, four rectangles B
   2½″ × 4½″ (7.5 cm × 11.5 cm)
   Blue fabric, eight squares C as connectors
   2½″ (7.5 cm)
   Red print, one square D
   4½″ (11.5 cm)

2. Make star points by stitching two blue connectors to ends of a yellow rectangle. Repeat to make four units.

3. Stitch a yellow square to each end of a two-connector unit. Stitch the other two connector units to opposite sides of red center square. Press seam allowances toward squares. Place all three rows of star in order, and stitch together. Make 10 stars.

Making a Strippy Set

4. To make outside triangles, cut four 13″ (34 cm) squares from print fabric. Cut each in half twice diagonally. For corner triangles, cut four 7″ (18 cm) print squares in half once diagonally. All triangles will be a little oversize, allowing you to square up edges after assembly.

5. This is a vertical, or "strippy," set. Each star block is finished with outside triangles or corner triangles, or a combination of them, so that it sits up straight in the quilt. Study layout diagram to determine where each triangle should go. Outside triangles are stitched to opposite sides of star block. On top and bottom blocks, an outside triangle and a corner block are sewn to opposite sides, and another corner triangle is sewn to a third side. After triangles have been joined to each star block, sew units together to make star strip. Bases of triangles will form straight sides of star strips. Trim to make a smooth edge if necessary. Leave a ¼″ (0.75 cm) seam allowance at corners of star blocks so they will not be blunted as construction continues.

6. Cut a 7½″ (19 cm) wide strip of print fabric in a length equal to star strips. Sew it lengthwise between star strips.

Borders

7. For inside borders, cut two side border strips of same length from same fabric 3½″ (9 cm) wide. Top and bottom borders will equal measurement across center of quilt with borders attached. Sew side borders on first and then top and bottom borders.

8. Outside borders are cut 5″ (12.5 cm) wide. Length for side borders equals center measurement of quilt with top and bottom borders attached. Sew side borders in place. Measure across center for length of top and bottom borders. Sew them in place.

Quilting

9. To add batting and backing, see page 155. Quilting by piece is recommended for star points and background of star. However, center of each star can be decorated with concentric circles of quilting or with a stitched star. Birds and leaves of two fabulous prints of borders can be highlighted with outline quilting; metallic thread would be very effective. Binding for this quilt is a bright blue print that picks up a color in both of prints of borders and of star points. See page 158 for instructions on binding quilt.

A home without a woman is like
a barn without cattle.

—Ethiopian proverb

Woman Warrior

◀ **WOMAN WARRIOR**
  by Kaye England, 1999. 60″ × 60″
  (152 cm × 152 cm).

This beautiful quilt is based on a simple layout of three side-by-side panels. The center panel is distinctive with a unique silk-screened motif depicting a woman's head, an apple, and a serpent. The individual motifs were cut from the panel and rearranged so that some of the sinuous curves would break the edges of the vertical set. As impressive as the appliquéd motif is, the quilt would be beautiful even if no exotic centerpiece were available. Any combination of pieced blocks and border-printed fabrics could run through the center of the quilt, as could a large motif of any design that pleases you.

T hat intrepid newspaper reporter and explorer, Henry Morton Stanley, writes in his journal of Amazon warriors:

> They may see Mtesa (the Emperor) drilling his Amazons and playing at soldiers. . . . They are all comely and brown, with fine virginal bosoms. But what strikes us most is the effect of discipline. Those timid and watchful eyes which they cast upon the monarch to discover his least wish prove that, though they may be devoted to him, it is evident that they have witnessed other scenes than those of love.[1]

In the history and literature of Africa, the term *Amazon* seems to be generic for "woman warrior," rather than for a specific group. One of the fiercest corps of the Fon army of Dahomey, dreaded as armed marauders by all their neighbors, was formed solely of women, who became known to Europeans as Amazons. They helped to conquer Yorubaland in the nineteenth century.

Women warriors were also part of the Zulu army under Shaka (see page IX). Part of his strategy for dealing with conquered clans was to incorporate its youth into his army; the women he captured formed female regiments, which became famous for their fighting ability: they have also been called "Amazons."

Even when they were not part of an elite fighting force, women across most of Africa have ordinarily enjoyed a role as an equal partner in the family. They usually have their own sphere of work, and have maintained a measure of independence and power. In most societies, girls are given lots of freedom and are spoiled and doted upon from infancy through adolescence. Only after the initiation rites into adulthood do they assume the responsibilities of contributing members of the group.

This brass casting of a deceased Queen Mother was done by the Yoruba of Benin in the sixteenth century and probably stood on an altar in the royal palace that was dedicated to high-ranking female ancestors. Her face shows the deliberate scarification practiced among many African women and no doubt provided some indication of her status and rank, which was equal to that of a town chief. Another indication of her rank is the crown of coral beads she is wearing; besides her, only the king and the chief warrior were allowed the privilege of such a headdress. Hers covers her hair, which has been dressed in a style known as the "chicken's beak." Photograph copyright © The British Museum.

Although the Islamic societies of North Africa generally restrict women's freedom more than the sub-Saharan peoples, there are exceptions. The Tuareg of north Africa even allow divorce. It is the man who has to leave, because the tent belongs to the woman, through inheritance. However, if the husband does not want the divorce, the woman (and her new lover, if she has one) must outrun the husband in a race to her tent. If the husband wins the race, they stay married.

Some mythical roles for women make them equal to men. For example, female as well as male ancestors are revered. Native religions honor many female spirits and goddesses. In many cultures, the role historically accorded to the mother of a king made her practically a sacred figure.

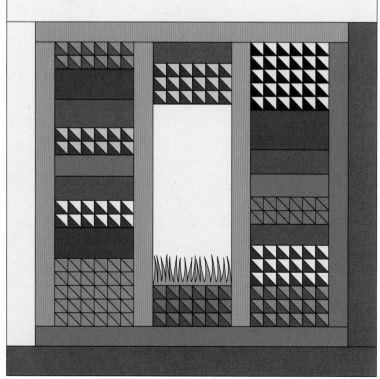

Layout diagram

Making Woman Warrior

FABRIC REQUIREMENTS

Based on 42" to 44" (106 cm to 112 cm) selvage to selvage

Mask border fabric A	2½ yd (370 cm)
Woman motif fabric B	3 yd (460 cm)
Environmental border fabric C	2½ yd (140 cm)
Assortment of 12 fabrics for pieced blocks, each	½ yd (45 cm)
Sashing and inside borders	¾ yd (70 cm)
Outside borders, each of two prints	1 yd (90 cm)
Backing	3½ yd (320 cm)
Binding	½ yd (45 cm)

Quick Piecing Half-Square Triangles

Notice that six color schemes are used for this quilt, and there are always five rows of six blocks, even though they may be presented in clusters of two or three rows of six blocks, or all together in five rows of six blocks. The width always stays the same, but the number of rows changes. However, somewhere in the piece, a total of six rows of each color scheme will be found. So you need 30 blocks of each color scheme. Study the photograph to see how to group the half-triangle squares into rows.

This method precludes cutting out triangles and stitching them together.

1. Determine size of square that two triangles will make when sewed together. In "Woman Warrior" the finished square measures 2" (5 cm). To finished size of square add ⅞" (2.5 cm). Count the number of squares you will need: in this case, there are 36 squares of each of six color schemes. Repeat steps 2 to 3 for each color scheme.

2. Cut two large rectangles, one from each of the two fabrics you are using. They should measure about 18" × 22" (45 cm × 55 cm). Anything larger is difficult to handle. On wrong side of lighter-colored of two fabrics, mark a grid. Make a series of horizontal lines 2⅞" (7.5 cm) apart; then cross them with a series of vertical lines 2⅞" (7.5 cm) apart. Draw a set of diagonal lines across the fabric that go precisely through each intersection of horizontal and vertical lines. These are cutting lines.

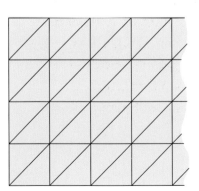

Step 2

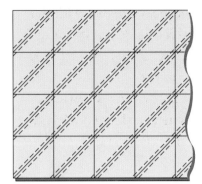

Step 3

3. Place right side of marked rectangle of fabric to right side of unmarked rectangle of fabric. Pin the two together, keeping pins away from diagonal lines. With sewing machine, stitch exactly ¼″ (0.75 cm) on both sides of diagonal lines, using a 12-15 stitch length. It is easier to stitch all lines on one side of diagonals first and then go back and stitch all lines on other side. If your presser foot cannot be used to accurately gauge a ¼″ (0.75 cm) stitching line, mark stitching lines with a nonpermanent marker or with stitching tape.

4. Cut through both layers of fabric on every one of the lines that you drew. You will have a number of squares, each made of two triangles, all exactly alike. Before you press all your little squares, clip off the corners at the end of each seam. Open square and press flat, seam allowances open.

Making a "Strippy" or Vertical Set

5. Once you've made six rows of half-triangle squares in the six different color schemes and grouped them in twos, threes, or whatever is needed, it's time to intersperse those blocks with strips of border prints. Arrange blocks and strips as desired to have three panels of the same length, 42½″ (106.5 cm).

TECHNIQUE

This "strippy," or vertical, set is enhanced by the overlapping of motifs from the body of the quilt onto the sashing strips, and by incorporating sashing fabric in the body of the quilt, making a totally integrated quilt. This integration is seen in the apple/serpent motif, which was left unstitched until the sashing was in place, although the other areas, including the woman's face, had been stitched down to the center panel. After the sashing was attached, the remainder of the motif was appliquéd. The integration is also seen in the row of grass across the bottom of the picture panel. It is cut freehand with the rotary cutter from the sashing fabric, then raw-edge appliquéd in place. You will see that you actually cut two rows of grasses, because the negative image is as good as the positive image.

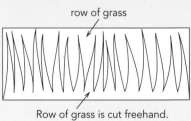

row of grass

Row of grass is cut freehand.

If you're crazy about border-printed fabrics and are always looking for a way to use them in your work, this quilt is for you. Alternating bands of border-printed fabrics and pieced blocks make up each of the three panels of the quilt. As shown, the quilt uses three different border prints: one with masks, one with black women and white women holding hands, and a third with an environmental motif that appears to be a horizon defined by a leafy vine. The pieced blocks are done in six color schemes, in a regular sequence: six motifs make up a row, and each row is repeated five times. In some cases, as in the upper right and lower left, all six rows are used together; in other instances, the rows are divided into groups of two and three. Choose African-themed fabrics, such as a tan and gray cheetah print matched with a red-orange "earth" print. Or a hot pink "cave drawing" print with a yellow, orange, and beige "earth" print.

6. When panels have been assembled, put them together with the grassy-type fabric used for sashing and for inside border for quilt. Cut two strips 4″ × 42½″ (8 cm × 106.5 cm) and sew them to pieced panels, alternating sashing with panels.

7. To determine length required for top and bottom 4″-wide grassy-type borders, measure across center of the quilt. Cut to this length and sew in place at top and bottom of quilt.

Borders

8. Top and sides of quilt are bordered in a light-colored print, unlike any fabric in quilt body. Bottom border is a one-directional border print of black women and white women holding hands. All borders are cut 5″ (13 cm) wide. Sides are approximately 49½″ (24 cm) long. Top and bottom are approximately 59½″ (149 cm) long. Exact measurements will be determined by size desired for quilt, which may vary considerably according to the width of border prints used.

Quilting

9. To add batting and backing, see page 155. While most of this quilt is outline-quilted to emphasize its precise piecing, decoration of this quilt surface does not stop there. Each triangle is also quilted in a meandering loop. Curves of the serpent, woman's face, the apple, all masks, and any fabric motifs are echoed with machine quilting. Lower inside border is enhanced with a vine made of beautiful yarns couched in place with metallic threads and finished with appliquéd leaves cut from environmental border. Trade beads in the form of faces add texture and interest; cutout masks from a border fabric dance gaily across and down two borders, subtly reinforcing the theme of faces begun in center panel. More surface embellishment can be applied after quilting and binding have been completed. See page 158 for instructions on binding the quilt.

The ruin of a nation begins in the homes of its people.

—Ashanti proverb

Life Is Not What You Expect

In most African belief systems, death is a great event, and it is handled through clearly defined rituals that announce the departure of the person's spirit to the next world and enabling that spirit to travel smoothly. Interestingly, textiles play an important part.

To announce that someone has died in the Ebira villages of the Niger River plain, lengths of specially woven blue and white striped fabric are hung by the front door of the deceased's house. The body is wrapped in other specially ordained indigo and white textiles for burial underneath the front veranda. The use of caskets for such entombments has come about only since Christianity has been influential, in the last 150 years or so. (One can't help recalling the burials in quilts on the trails in the settlement of the western United States.)

The Yoruba of Nigeria also drape the exterior of houses where an important man lies in state awaiting burial. A textile that looks like an excessively long, intricately woven bellpull runs from the front door, up across the steeply sloping thatched roof, to the other side of the house. At the peak of the roof, woven cloths of a complex red and white pattern are spread, indicating the high prestige of the departed. These burial cloths are also used in the masquerades that commemorate the deceased elder. Relics from the honored man are incorporated into the performance garb as a sign of respect.

The use of appliqué in shrines at the grave of a loved one is well established and demonstrates that the skills used to make articles for other ceremonies were also applied to accessories for funerals. Wood carving, one of the best known of all African crafts, is often applied to making funerary posts. These posts, carved to represent a specific personality in figurative rather than literal imagery, may be placed in front of a dwelling or around the gravesite, according to the practices of the particular group. Some groups believe that an ancestor can approach a living relative and actually ask that one of these

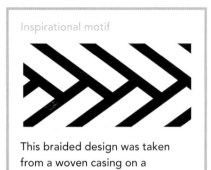

This braided design was taken from a woven casing on a Congolese casket.

commemorative posts be erected to him, much as the living ask the departed for their help. To those who believe in ancestor worship, the communication runs both ways.

This braid design, well known in many cultures, was found on a woven casket lining from the Congo. The departed ancestors of each family in the Mbole clan (all of whom carry the same totemic name, such as "turtle" or "thunder") are represented on the decorated woven mats that are displayed at important occasions, much like family banners. The mats are buried with elders of the clan. It is highly likely that the casket lining from which this braid motif was taken was a Mbole mat.

There is nothing funerary about either of the quilts included here, and both make excellent use of the braid design. Although it has long been popular as a border for quilts, the braid also works well as an overall quilt pattern. Both of the quilts shown here contain several great ideas for borders.

◀ AFRICAN BRAID

◀ **AFRICAN BRAID**

by the Cayman Island Quilters,
quilted by Mary Jane Parvey, 1999.
62″ × 62″ (157 cm × 157 cm).
Collection of Kaye England.

The braid design, with the addition of a
repeated black square, has been used to
make an entire quilt top. A wonderfully
broad selection of African-themed fabrics
has been used in this quilt and again in
the "Roman Stripe" and "Flying Geese"
borders.

Making Life Is Not What You Expect

FABRIC REQUIREMENTS

Based on 42″ to 44″ (106 cm to 112 cm) selvage to selvage

It's not really possible to give accurate yardage requirements for this quilt, because its elements are so flexible. The braid design is the focus; it is made of a number of African fabrics. Choose a selection that gives you the color range you want and cut them into strips that are 2½″ × 18″ (6.5 cm × 45 cm). In addition, ½ yd (45 cm) of black fabric should be plenty to cut 1¼″ (4 cm) strips in 18″ (45 cm) lengths to equal the number of colored strips you have.

Making the Braid Design

1. With right sides together, sew each black strip lengthwise to a colored strip. Press seam allowances toward black strip. Now you will have a long colored strip that is bordered on one side with black. Cut strip into 6″ (15 cm) long "bricks."

2. The first seam sets the shape of the braid. To make it, place two "bricks" right sides together, with one perpendicular to the other. Stitch as shown; then finger press to form a "V" with the black strips on inside.

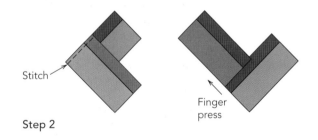

Stitch

Finger press

Step 2

3. Sew another "brick" beneath two that are joined. Press "brick" down, away from braid.

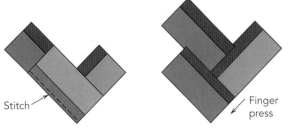

Stitch

Finger press

Step 3

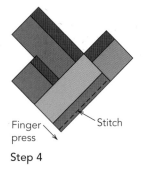

Finger press → | Stitch

Step 4

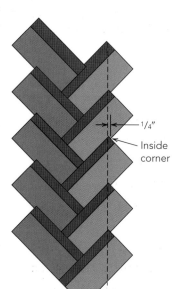

1/4" — | — Inside corner

Step 6

4. Add a "brick" to other side of braid as shown. Stitch in place. Press down.

5. Continue adding "bricks" alternately to each side of braid until desired length is reached. Take care to place colors correctly so that a narrow black strip alternates with a wide colored strip.

6. When finished, edges of braid strip will be stair-stepped. Do not trim them until after strip has been sewn to another piece, because the resulting long bias edge is very stretchy. Seamline will be ¼" (0.75 cm) from inside corners. (*Note:* In quilt shown, braid is joined directly to a pieced border on both sides; after that joining has been made, ends of "bricks" can be trimmed evenly.)

Borders

7. An inside border is included only on top and bottom of quilt. Cut two 1½"-wide strips of black fabric in a length to equal measurement of quilt top across center. Sew in place. Press.

8. Outside borders are made from two traditional quilt patterns, in same fabrics as "bricks." Two sides are bordered in "Flying Geese" and two in "Roman Stripe." All four border strips finish to 4" × 68" (10 cm × 173 cm). Make as many "Flying Geese" units (page 125) as needed to complete two border strips; then make three more to place randomly in one of the "Roman Stripe" border strips. "Roman Stripe" is made by simply sewing 4½"-wide (11.25 cm) strips of varying lengths together until a total length of 68" (173 cm) is reached. Make one strip of nothing but fabric strips. Make second in same way, but insert three "Flying Geese" blocks as desired.

Quilting

9. To add batting and backing, see page 155. This quilt has been machine-quilted in a meandering pattern, using metallic thread. See page 158 for instructions on binding quilt.

Finishing the Quilt

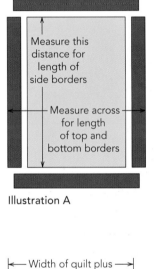

Illustration A

Illustration B

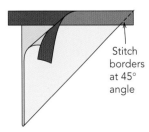

Illustration C

Applying Borders

There are two types of borders. Square borders can be applied by attaching the border strips to opposite sides of the quilt, then across the top and bottom. You choose the width. The length of the side borders equals the length of the quilt. The length of the top and bottom borders equals the width of the quilt including the side borders (Illustration A).

Mitered borders are more appropriate when a stripe is used or when you will appliqué on top of the border. Cut the border strips for all sides, using a length equal to the quilt dimension plus two additional border widths, plus seam allowances. Sew the borders to the quilt, centering them lengthwise on each side so that the excess is evenly distributed between the two ends of the quilt. Do not sew the borders to one another yet (Illustration B).

Fold the quilt in half diagonally, right sides together, placing the two borders right sides together. Arrange borders so raw horizontal edges are matched, and mark a 45-degree angle across the borders by extending the fold line. Stitch on the marked line (Illustration C). Trim away excess border fabric. Repeat the process for all four corn

Basting the Quilt "Sandwich"

Begin making the quilt "sandwich" by preparing the backing of the quilt. You may seam the back together with one seam down the center, but the design possibilities are increased if you use two seams. This allows you to have three panels, and those panels can be made of as many segments as you wish. There's no reason not to have a fine back on your quilt. Just make sure it is a bit larger all around than the quilt top. It is wise to make the backing and batting at least 3″

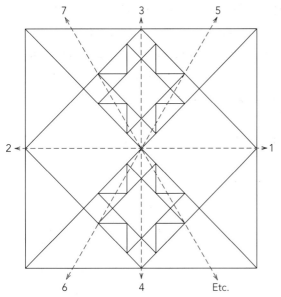

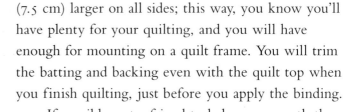

Illustration D

(7.5 cm) larger on all sides; this way, you know you'll have plenty for your quilting, and you will have enough for mounting on a quilt frame. You will trim the batting and backing even with the quilt top when you finish quilting, just before you apply the binding.

If possible, get a friend to help you smooth the back out flat and tape it to the floor with masking tape. Smooth the quilt batting out over the backing; it should also be a bit larger all around than the top.

Finally, lay your quilt top, with the borders attached, right side up over the batting. When you are sure it is perfectly in place, you can baste.

Baste from the center to the opposite sides, then from the center to the top and bottom, then from the center to the corners. If necessary, add more basting lines between each of these, always working from the center, first in one direction, then in the opposite direction (Illustration D). Use a large running stitch—that's what basting is, after all.

A good tip is to start at the center with a long thread, and baste to one side, leaving a long thread "tail" at the center. Rethread the needle and baste to the opposite side. Or, you can secure the basting stitches at the center with a backstitch.

(*Note:* If you are planning to machine-quilt your piece, you can substitute safety pins for thread basting.)

Quilting

You must make a number of creative decisions when you are ready to quilt your piece. One of the first is whether you want to do it by hand or by machine. Machine quilting is standard now on fine quilts, because it can create effects that cannot be achieved any other way. One of the best looks for African quilts is a meandering pattern done in metallic thread. Many of the quilts in this book are quilted by machine, using variegated metallic thread. Mary Jane Parvey, who quilts for Kaye on a recent-vintage home sewing machine, uses a technique she calls "prequilting." She uses a Sulky invisible thread to stitch "in the ditch" with a walking foot, and she straight-stitches the major seams of the quilt top this way. Once the entire quilt is prequilted, Mary Jane then decides which areas she wants to highlight with a machine quilting pattern, and she chooses the thread for the effect she wants. On some quilts, she uses four or five different threads. Often with metallic or bulky threads she uses a lightweight cotton thread in the bobbin. She experiments on scrap pieces, duplicating the layers of the quilt, until she is confident that the stitching will produce the effect she wants on the finished quilt.

You are not, of course, limited to meandering overall patterns for machine quilting. However, if you want to use a regular pattern, you have to transfer the quilting design onto the quilt top just as you do for hand-quilting. Following are some directions from Holice Turnbow, who designed the quilting patterns beginning on page 165.

Transferring the Quilting Design

The design can be transferred to the quilt top in two ways—by template or stencil. If the design has little detail (such as "Strength" or "Faith" in the following selection), a template can be made and used to mark the design.

Making a Template

1. Trace or make a copy of the design.
2. Transfer the design to a sheet of lightweight plastic or cardboard.
3. Cut out the design using scissors or a craft knife. The craft knife may be more useful if the design has an inner section that needs to be cut out.
4. If you intend to use the template over an extended period of time, you can glue fine sandpaper on the back of the cardboard or plastic to prevent the template from moving when marking.

Making a Stencil

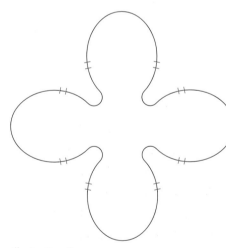

Illustration E

Only three items are needed for making a quilting stencil: double-blade cutting knife, a sheet of flexible plastic, and a rotary cutting mat. There are two double-blade knives available. One is manufactured by Olfa products and the other by Griffith. Both are available through quilt shops and craft stores. A flexible plastic sheet is necessary because it is difficult to cut the thin, stiff plastic normally used for templates. A product manufactured especially for stencils is DBK Plastic, available in quilt shops. This plastic is soft and easy to cut with a double-blade knife.

1. Trace or make a copy of the design.
2. Mark where "bridges" should be left in the stencil (Illustration E). These bridges are necessary to keep the stencil from falling apart. Cuts should not be more than 2 inches (5 cm) in length. Longer cuts often cause the stencil to lose stability and make it difficult to mark the pattern on the quilt.
3. Trim away excess paper on your design, leaving a margin of about ½″ to 1″ (1.25 cm to 2.5 cm) all around. Mark the design directly

on the plastic with a fine-line permanent marking pen, or place the design underneath the plastic and tape it temporarily in place.

4. Hold the double-blade knife at about a 45-degree angle and make short cuts along the design lines. Be sure to apply equal pressure to both blades or you will cut only one side of the channel.

5. Clip the ends of each channel of plastic and remove. Continue to cut until all lines of the stencil are marked with a channel.

6. Place the stencil on the quilt top and mark the fabric through the channels with a quilter's pencil or chalk. If the markings are easier to see, you may want to connect them with a continuous line.

Binding

Cut strips of fabric 2½″ (6.5 cm) wide and long enough to go completely around the outside edge of your quilt, with about two additional inches for overlap. Binding need not be cut on the bias unless the fabric design (e.g., stripes) looks better on the bias. Binding works perfectly well cut on the straight grain, and it takes less fabric. Fold the binding in half, without pressing, and place on the quilt top, raw edges aligned. Sew through all layers of the sandwiched quilt— top, batting, and backing—with a ¼″ (0.75 cm) seam allowance. Fold the binding over the raw edges of the quilt sandwich to the back of the quilt and slipstitch into place.

To turn corners, sew to within ¼″ (0.75 cm) of the edge, then turn the binding up, folding it at a 45-degree angle.

Fold the binding back down straight so the second fold is even with the stitched edge of the quilt and the binding is in place along the other edge of the quilt. Continue sewing down the second side of the binding. This will give you a folded miter rather than a stitched miter.

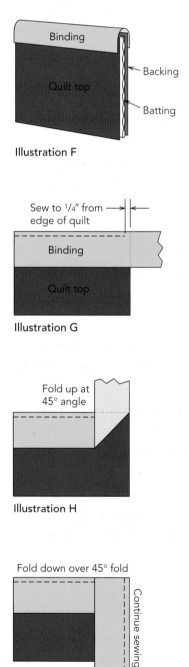

Illustration F

Illustration G

Illustration H

Illustration I

Sources for African Fabrics and Embellishments

St. Theresa Textile Trove

1329 Main Street

Cincinnati, OH 45210

Becky Hancock, proprietor

513-333-0300

www.stheresatextiletrove.com

When it comes to finding African things, there's no better resource than Becky Hancock. Her stock of beads and charms will inspire anybody to make quilts just so they will have something to embellish. Best of all, everything is authentic. Becky travels frequently to all parts of Africa and South America to buy; she is married to a West African (from Gambia) and is a great source of stories and travel tales.

Homeland Fabrics/IBN, Inc.

122 West 27th Street

New York, NY 10001

Abdoulaye Diaw, Vice President

212-367-8779 (telephone)

212-367-9290 (facsimile)

This company is the largest importer of African fabrics in the United States and exhibits at Quilt Market in Houston. Contact them to find where you can buy authentic African fabrics in your area. When Kaye fretted to Abdoulaye, who is a native of Ghana, about whether we would be taken seriously doing a book like this, he reassured her in his melodious accent, "It is not necessary that you live in Africa—it is only necessary that you love it." We certainly qualify on that score.

African Images

7301 Ginger Spice Lane

Charlotte, NC 28227

Mamadou and Barbara Frantao, Proprietors

704-545-9796 (telephone)

704-545-6763 (facsimile)

This company imports fabrics, mud cloth clothing, jewelry, arts, and accessories. Mamadou is from Mali, and he and Barbara make frequent trips back to his homeland to buy fabrics and other items for the American market. Contact them if you are interested in buying authentic African fabrics. They will send you a swatch list with current prices. African fabrics come in precut lengths, and you usually cannot obtain additional yardage. Buy what you want when you see it. It may be available only once. Mamadou and Barbara hasten to caution customers about this aspect of imported fabrics.

South Sea Imports

550 West Artesia Boulevard   800-829-0066 (telephone)
Compton, CA 90220   310-763-4777 (facsimile)

South Sea Imports is a fabric manufacturing company that began as an import company, which explains the name. It produces Kaye England's fabric lines, "Matters of the Heart," some of which are named "Festival of Colors," "Festival of Colors Too," and "African Inspirations"; all are African-themed designs. Kaye's lines always include wonderful background fabrics in textures that represent grass, stone, water, baskets, and birds or other animals, as well as geometrics and border prints that can be cut to create many different looks. She does great novelty prints as well, focusing on motifs that speak immediately to us of Africa. Look for her fabrics in your local quilt or fabric shop, or call to learn where you might look in your area.

The Stencil Company

28 Castlewood Drive   716-656-9430 (telephone)
Cheektowaga, NY 14227   716-668-2488 (facsimile)
www.quiltingstencils.com (website)   stencil@webt.com (E-mail)

If you don't want to go to the trouble of making your own quilting stencils from the designs by Holice Turnbow included in this book, you can order stencils from the special African series designed by him for The Stencil Company, which is owned by Holice's daughter Cindy and has an inventory of several hundred other designs as well. Although Holice has worked with The Stencil Company since its beginning in the mid-1980s, he now concentrates primarily on designing the stencils they produce. He has been quilting since the mid-1970s and is well known in the quilting world, not only for his professional teaching and judging but also for his big heart and his humanitarian works. Holice's time in Africa informed the quilting designs he produced especially for this book and gave him insight into the names he selected for each.

Selected Bibliography

We suggest that you go to the library or the bookstore and pick out books on Africa that address not only the art of the continent, although there are many beautiful books on the subject, but also those that offer a panorama of Africa's natural beauty and its peoples. There is much to inspire you. Also, lest you get lost in ancient Africa, look for sources that show Africa as it is today, and look for perspectives that are not necessarily American. Don't overlook archaeology and anthropology resources if your questions are not being fully answered elsewhere. There are many components to the subject of Africa. Following are some of the sources we particularly enjoyed.

Aardema, Verna. *Misoso: Once Upon a Time: Tales from Africa.* New York, 1994, Knopf.

Abrahams, Roger D. *African Folktales.* New York, 1983, Pantheon.

Adler, Peter, and Nicholas Barnard. *African Majesty—The Textile Art of the Ashanti & Ewe.* New York, 1992, Thames and Hudson.

———. *Asafo! African Flags of the Fante.* New York, 1991, Thames and Hudson.

Algotsson, Sharne, and Denys David. *The Spirit of African Design.* New York, 1996, Clarkson Potter.

Anderson, Martha G., and Christine Mullen Kreamer. *Wild Spirits, Strong Medicine: African Art and the Wilderness.* Seattle, 1989, University of Washington Press.

Atmore, Anthony, and Gillian Stacey. *Black Kingdoms, Black Peoples: The West African Heritage.* Photographs by Werner Forman. London, 1979, Orbis Publishing.

Ayo, Yvonne. *Africa.* New York, 1995, Knopf.

Beckwith, Carol, and Angela Fisher. *African Ark.* New York, 1990, Abrams.

Blier, Suzanne Preston. *The Royal Arts of Africa: The Majesty of Form.* New York, 1998, Abrams.

Caraway, Caren. *African Designs of the Congo, the Guinea Coast, and Nigeria and the Cameroons.* Owings Mills, Maryland, 1994, Stemmer House.

Chanda, Jacqueline. *African Arts and Cultures.* Worcester, Massachusetts, 1993, Davis.

Clarke, Duncan. *African Art.* New York, 1995, Crescent Books.

————. *African Hats and Jewelry.* Edison, New Jersey, 1998, Chartwell Books.

————. *The Art of African Textiles.* San Diego, California, 1997, Thunder Bay Press.

Courtney-Clark, Margaret. *Ndebele: The Art of an African Tribe.* New York, 1986, Rizzoli.

Dempsey, Robert (editor). *Stencils.* Glenview, Illinois, 1993, Goodyear.

Devine, Elizabeth, and Nancy L. Braganti. *The Traveler's Guide to African Customs & Manners.* New York, 1995, St. Martin's.

Diallo, Siradiou. *Zaire Today.* Paris, 1977, Editions Jeune Afriqué.

Duchateau, Armand. *Benin, Royal Art of Africa.* Munich, 1994, Prestel.

Ellis, George W. *Negro Culture in West Africa.* New York, 1914, Neale Publishing.

Finlay, Hugh, *et al. Africa on a Shoestring.* Oakland, California, 1998, Lonely Planet Publications.

Fisher, Angela. *Africa Adorned.* New York, 1984, Abrams.

Gibson, Clare. *Signs and Symbols.* New York, 1966, Barnes and Noble.

Gordon, René. *Africa Revealed.* New York, 1981, St. Martin's.

————. *Africa, The Art of a Continent: 100 Works of Power and Beauty.* New York, 1995, The Guggenheim Museum.

Haskins, James, and Kathleen Benson. *African Beginnings.* New York, 1998, Lothrop, Lee & Shepard.

Haskins, Jim, and Joann Biondi. *From Afar to Zulu: A Dictionary of African Cultures.* New York, 1995, Walker.

Horton, Roberta. *The Fabric Makes the Quilt.* Lafayette, California, 1995, C&T Publishing.

Johns, Christopher. *Valley of Life, Africa's Great Rift.* Virginia, 1991, Thomasson-Grant.

Jordan, Manuel (editor). *Chokwe! Art and Initiation Among Chokwe and Related Peoples.* Munich, 1998, Prestel.

Kertscher, Kevin. *Africa Solo: A Journey Across the Sahara, Sahel, and Congo.* South Royalton, Vermont, 1998, Steerforth.

King, Noel Q. *Religions of Africa: A Pilgrimage into Traditional Religions.* New York, 1970, Harper and Row.

Kingsolver, Barbara. *The Poisonwood Bible.* New York, 1998, Harper Collins.

Knappert, Jan. *African Mythology.* London, 1995, Diamond Books.

Knight, Natalie, and Suzanne Priebatsch. *Art of the Ndebele: The Evolution of a Cultural Identity.* Johannesburg and Toronto, 1998, Natalie Knight.

————. *Ndebele Images.* Johannesburg and Toronto, 1983, Natalie Knight.

LaDuke, Betty. *Africa: Women's Art, Women's Lives.* Trenton, New Jersey, 1997, Africa World Press.

Mack, John. *Emil Torday and The Art of the Congo.* Seattle, Washington, University of Washington Press [no date].

Mack, John, (editor). *Masks and the Art of Expression.* New York, 1994, Abrams.

Marc, Alexandre. *African Art: The World Bank Collection.* Washington, D.C., 1998, The World Bank.

Matthiessen, Peter. *The Tree Where Man Was Born.* New York, 1972, MJF Books.

Maybury-Lewis, David. *Millennium: Tribal Wisdom and the Modern World.* New York, 1992, Viking.

McGeary, Johanna, and Marguerite Michaels. "Africa Rising," *Time,* March 30, 1998.

Meyer, Laure. *Art and Craft in Africa: Everyday Life, Ritual, Court Art.* Paris, 1994 (English edition 1995), Finest S.A. /Editions Pierre Terrail.

Miller, Barbara. *Tuareg.* Danbury, Connecticut, 1995, Grolier Educational.

Mirow, Gregory. *Traditional African Designs.* Mineola, New York, 1997, Dover.

Mountfield, David. *A History of African Exploration.* Northbrook, Illinois, 1976, Domus Books. (Originally published in United Kingdom by Hamlyn Publishing, Feltham, Middlesex, 1976.)

Murray, Jocelyn (editor). *Cultural Atlas of Africa.* Oxford, 1981, Equinox, and New York, 1981, Facts on File.

Nooter, Mary H. *Secrecy: African Art That Conceals and Reveals.* New York and Munich, 1993, The Museum for African Art and Prestel.

Nowell-Smith, Geoffrey. *Explorers and Exploration,* Volume 8, *Africa and Arabia.* Danbury, Connecticut, 1998, Grolier Educational.

Ollivier, John J. *The Wisdom of African Mythology.* Largo, Florida, 1994, Top of the Mountain Publications.

Parrinder, Geoffrey. *African Mythology.* New York, 1996, Barnes and Noble.

Picton, John, and John Mack. *African Textiles.* New York, 1989, Harper and Row.

Powell, Ivor (author), and Mark Lewis (photographer). *Ndebele: A People and Their Art.* New York and London, 1995, Cross River Press.

Reader, John. *Africa: A Biography of the Continent.* New York, 1999, Knopf.

Schulthess, Emil. *Africa.* New York, 1959, Simon and Schuster.

———. *Isak Dinesen's Africa.* San Francisco, 1985, Sierra Club Books.

Stanley, Diane, and Peter Vennema. *Shaka, King of the Zulus.* New York, 1988, Morrow Junior Books.

Stanley, Henry M. *Through the Dark Continent.* Volume 1, Mineola, New York, 1988, Dover. (Originally published in London by G. Newnes, 1899.)

Thompson, Robert Ferris. *Africa's Glorious Legacy.* Alexandria, Virginia, 1994, Time-Life.

———. *East Africa.,* Amsterdam, 1986, Time-Life.

———. *Face of the Gods: Art and Altars of Africa and the African Americas.* Munich, 1993, Prestel.

Vail, Pegi. *Omo Peoples.* Danbury, Connecticut, 1995, Grolier Educational.

van der Post, Laurens. *The Lost World of the Kalahari.* Photographs by David Coulson. New York and London, 1988, William Morrow, and Chatton & Windus.

van Wyck, Gary N. *African Painted Houses: Basotho Dwellings of Southern Africa.* New York, 1998, Abrams.

———. *Assuming the Guise: African Masks Considered and Reconsidered.* Williamstown, Massachusetts, 1991, Williams College Museum of Art.

Virel, André. *Decorated Man: The Human Body as Art.* Photographs by Charles and Josette Lenars; translated from the French by I. Mark Paris. New York, 1980, Abrams.

Williams, Geoffrey. *African Designs from Traditional Sources.* Mineola, New York, 1971, Dover.

Templates

Gyamu (JOW mu)
Symbol of courage
and determination

ADINKRA SYMBOLS

ADINKRA SYMBOLS

Mmra Krado
(mm RAH KRAH doh)
The seal of law and
order—a symbol of the
powers of the court

Kuntinkantan
(koon tin KAHN TAHN)
Symbol of humility and
servitude

ADINKRA
SYMBOLS

ADINKRA
SYMBOLS

ADINKRA SYMBOLS

Adinkrahene
(a DINK krah HAY nay)
A symbol of the chief
of the Adinkra

Gye nyame
(jee nyah MAY)
Immortality of God

ADINKRA SYMBOLS

Kojo baiden
(koh JOH BAY den)
Sun rays, the double
crescent moon and the
Asante stool—a symbol
of the universe

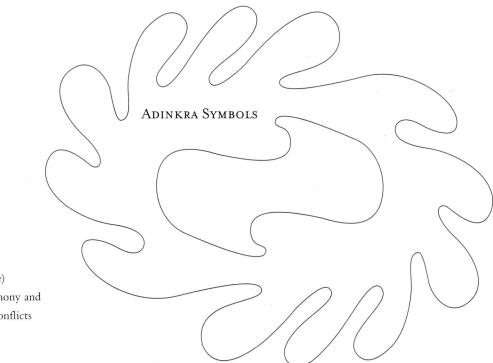

ADINKRA SYMBOLS

Binkabi
(been KAH bee)
Symbol of harmony and
unity—avoid conflicts

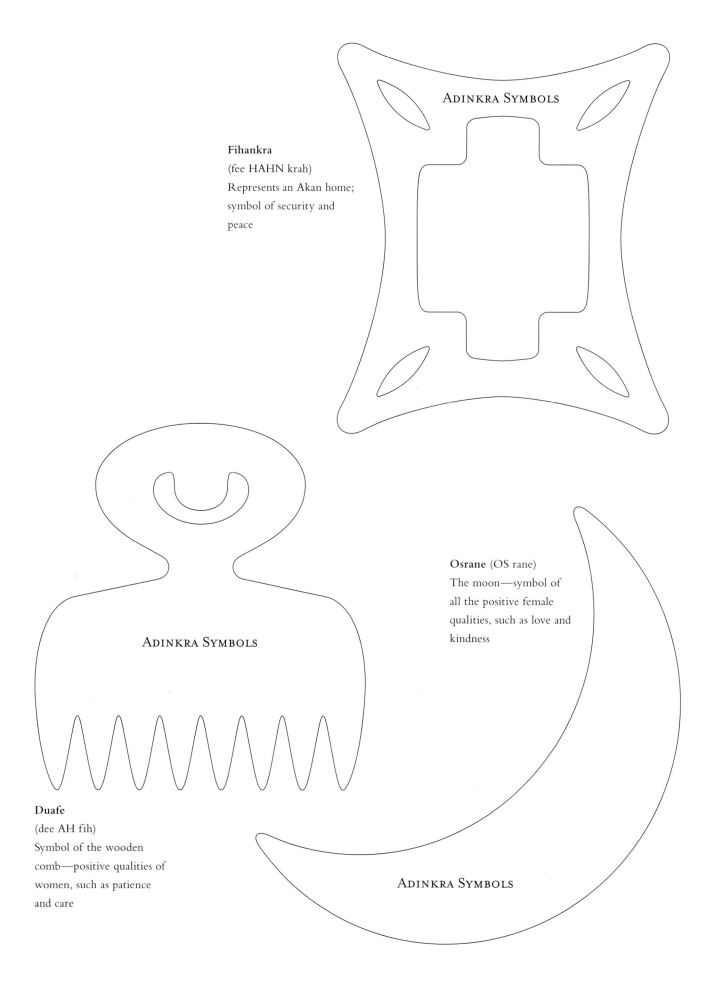

ADINKRA SYMBOLS

Fihankra
(fee HAHN krah)
Represents an Akan home;
symbol of security and
peace

Osrane (OS rane)
The moon—symbol of
all the positive female
qualities, such as love and
kindness

ADINKRA SYMBOLS

Duafe
(dee AH fih)
Symbol of the wooden
comb—positive qualities of
women, such as patience
and care

ADINKRA SYMBOLS

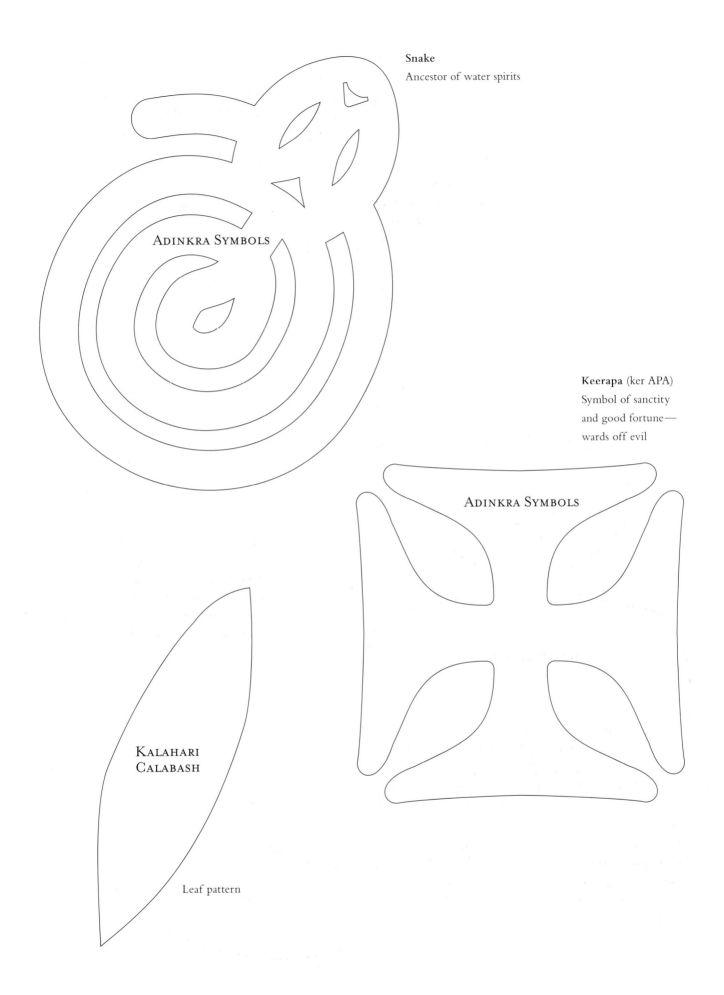

Snake
Ancestor of water spirits

ADINKRA SYMBOLS

Keerapa (ker APA)
Symbol of sanctity
and good fortune—
wards off evil

ADINKRA SYMBOLS

KALAHARI
CALABASH

Leaf pattern

African Quilting Designs

God's protection

Strength

Warning from jealousy

Greatness

Protection

Textile motif

Sunrise/moonset

Love and goodwill

Law and justice

Faith

Mask motif

Gateway

Shields

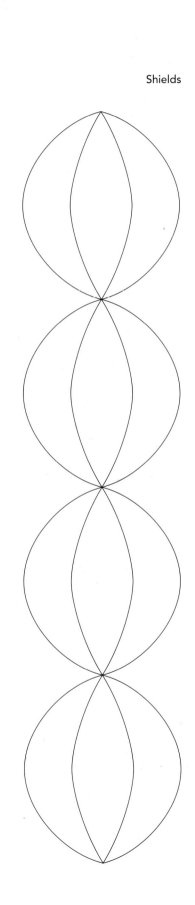

Protection

Pride

Wisdom

Security

High tide/
low tide

Wisdom and creativity

Diamonds